# THE
# CHAMPIONSHIP TABLE

# THE
# CHAMPIONSHIP
# TABLE

DANA **SMITH** · TOM **McEVOY** · RALPH **WHEELER**

# CARDOZA PUBLISHING

Cardoza Publishing is the foremost gaming publisher in the world, with a library of over 100 up-to-date and easy-to-read books and strategies. These authoritative works are written by the top experts in their fields and, with more than 7,000,000 books in print, represent the best-selling and most popular gaming books anywhere.

SECOND EDITION

Library of Congress Catalog Card No: 2003114970
ISBN:1-58042-125-3

Visit our new web site (www.cardozapub.com) or write us for a full list of Cardoza books, advanced and computer strategies.

CARDOZA PUBLISHING
P.O. Box 1500, Cooper Station, New York, NY 10276
Phone (800)577-WINS
email: cardozapub@aol.com
www.cardozapub.com

# Contents

# Acknowledgements

We gratefully acknowledge the many people who have helped us in researching and producing this book. When we needed hard-to-find information on the early World Series of Poker, Doyle Brunson was always just a phone call away. Puggy Pearson assisted us in identifying the people pictured in the 1974 and 1976 WSOP photographs that we were able to obtain with the kind assistance of Dr. David Schwartz at the University of Nevada, Las Vegas, and Karen War in the Lied Library at the university.

Larry Grossman, who has photographed players at the WSOP for many years, was most generous in sharing his photographs with us. Although you couldn't tell it, photography is only a hobby with Grossman. He has been the host of his own radio show, "You Can Bet On It," for many years and writes a column by the same name for *What's On* magazine in Las Vegas. He also is the author of a two-volumne set of books by the same title. His photographs hang on the walls at Gamblers Book Club in Las Vegas and in the poker room at Sunset Station Casino.

We appreciate the cooperation of the poker room management at Binion's Horseshoe in Las Vegas, and the staff at *Card Player* magazine, for assisting us further with the photographs reproduced in this book. The tedious job of compiling the index fell to Darlene Wood, co-author Smith's assistant at Cardsmith Publishing.

We extend our heartfelt thanks to Berry Johnston, T.J. Cloutier, Cowboy Wolford and Phil Hellmuth for helping us with the "How It Happened" reports.

# Foreword
## by Tom McEvoy

I have had a love affair with the World Series of Poker ever since I stumbled into Binion's Horseshoe in Las Vegas at the tail end of the 1978 championship event. There sat the crafty Bobby Baldwin with mounds of chips stacked in front of him playing heads up against a dapper gentleman in his early forties named Crandall Addington. Noticing the reaction of the crowd I drooped in awe, overwhelmed that poker was such a glamorous world that people were standing 12 deep just to get a glimpse of the finalists. I was still there when Baldwin captured the title.

When I saw that exciting finale in '78, I had not yet moved to Las Vegas to begin my professional poker career. Nevertheless I vowed to myself right then and there that within the next five years I would be a part of it all—which might have sounded a little brash at the time because I had never played a single hand of Texas hold'em at that point. I knew, however, that I would learn. Much to everyone's surprise, especially my own, five years later I not only played the championship event for the first time, I won it! I have been an avid fan and historian of the Series ever since, and I know that many of you share my ongoing love affair with it.

This book chronicles the World Champions of Poker from 1970 through 2003. It is laid out in chronological sequence with interviews from past champions and key contenders who narrowly missed the gold and the glory. You can sense their heartbreak when a cruel river card in one key hand, often the last hand, snatched victory from their grasp. We show you the final hand of each of the championship tournaments, and give you a description of how it was played that may help guide you in forming an opinion as to what you might have done if you had been at the championship table with Johnny or Doyle or Phil or Noel or Russ or Carlos.

I hope that all you poker fans will love reading about the premier gaming event in the world as much I have enjoyed contributing to this book. And who knows? In these pages you may find the inspiration that will lead you to the championship table at the World Series of Poker, where I hope to meet you once again.

# Introduction
### by Dana Smith

In a game where the plot is slow moving and the action is sporadic, it is the cast of characters that makes a poker tournament interesting enough to glue audiences to their seats. In the early days the cast at the World Series of Poker included some mighty colorful characters—Doyle "Texas Dolly" Brunson in his oversized Stetson radiating his unique brand of personal magnetism, Puggy Pearson garbed as Julius Caesar or Attila the Hun with his motor mouth racing at full speed, Amarillo Slim Preston wearing snakeskin, monogrammed boots grandstanding for the audience and shooting the bull with reporters and pretty women.

The Championship Table pays tribute to the poker players of the last three decades who have known the thrill of victory and suffered the agony of defeat in their quest to win the World Championship of Poker. From 1970 when a road gambler was voted the title and received a trophy as a memento, through 2003 when an accountant who won his entry into the tournament via an online satellite defeated 838 entrants and received $2.5 million for his victory, this book records the players who made it to the championship table, pictures the last hand between the champion and the runner-up, how they played their cards and how much they won.

Everything about the first years of the Series was amateur except the players—they all were professionals, most of them Texas road gamblers, migrant workers who plied their trade in smoky backrooms nestled along the dusty backroads of the Southern poker circuit. No events were actually scheduled and no one was formally invited, the word simply got around. "If seven 7-card stud players arrived at the Horseshoe at the same time, they'd play the 7-stud contest, provided one of them wasn't asleep," Eric Drache, director of the WSOP in the early days, observed. Just before the tournament began in 1973, Jack Binion and Jimmy "The Greek" Snyder were hustling to set up the tables and lay out the chips for the thirteen men who had paid to play the event. The 1983 video pictures the two finalists playing heads-up for $540,000 with their ladies seated alongside them at the table. A lot has changed since then.

We did not intend to write a complete history of the World Series of Poker, although our book is filled with enough facts about it to satisfy the curiosity of most WSOP buffs. We have included significant highlights from each Series that allow you to follow its growth from the six road gamblers who played it in 1970 to over one-hundred times that many players who entered it in 2003. Because our focus is the players, we scattered colorful quips and quotations throughout the book that add insight into how poker players think.

Seems like it should have been an easy task to track down the last hands, the board cards and how the finalists played their cards—wrong. It was a lot tougher than I ever imagined. To the rescue came Ralph Wheeler, devoted WSOP fan and historian, who conceived the idea for this book. For years he has clipped media reports about the Series, carefully organizing his data in voluminous notebooks. What Wheeler didn't know about the players or their cards Tom McEvoy did. McEvoy, a self-confessed Series junkie, has a thick album devoted to each championship event since 1978, including daily progress sheets and photos. Understandably, his largest album is from 1983, the year he won the Big One in the longest heads-up match ever played at the championship table. In a few cases we were unable to find pertinent information such as the exact suits or ranks of board cards and starting chip counts because no complete archival records appear to be available.

Over the years I have interviewed more than a hundred tournament poker players. Included in this book are some of their stories—tales of triumph and tribulation, exhilation and exasperation, stories of adventure told by players who have been there, done that, in the world of poker. Not all of them have won the Big One but they came mighty close. You may find yourself crying with them as they relate how it felt when the elusive butterfly of luck fluttered past them only to alight on the shoulder of the victor.

We particularly enjoyed researching the WSOP video tapes. They weren't all as professional as today's slick productions, the action wasn't always easy to follow, and sometimes there wasn't much of a story line. But each video contained a fascinating cast of characters. It is to that cast that we dedicate this book.

# 1970 World Championship Event
## 1st World Series of Poker
Number of Players: 38
Number of Games: 5

"In 1970 Benny Binion and his son Jack were of the firm belief that poker could be promoted as a competitive sport. They got a few of their big players together and had a social tournament. When it was over, the crafty Johnny Moss was declared the winner." This is how the 1984 World Series of Poker magazine-like brochure, published annually between 1983 and 1998, described the genesis of the WSOP. Johnny Moss, who later was dubbed the "Grand Old Man of Poker," was awarded the championship by a vote of his peers.

Journalist Phil Hevener chronicled the events that led up to the inaugural Series in more detail in the 1986 WSOP brochure: "Despite the precision with which it has moved from year to year as a carefully directed Happening, the events that gave birth to the World Series were not nearly so calculated.

"Las Vegas casino industry veteran Vic Vickrey was drafted by the former owners of the Holiday Hotel and Casino to see if he could pump some vitality into the Reno gambling hall after its 1967 purchase by a group of Texans headed by the late Tom Moore. Vickrey conceived what he envisioned as the 'Gaming Fraternity Convention' for a 'slow time of the year' and invited a group of Texas gamblers who might be expected to attend such a gathering.

"The Binions, including family patriarch Benny Binion and his son Jack were among them. Jack said later, 'This was the first time I had ever met Doyle Brunson.'

"Vickrey remembers that the 'Holiday had a couple of old poker tables over there in the corner, and I tossed in $3,000 of the hotel's money just so's these fellas would have a little somethin' extra to try shootin' at.'

"Vickrey found he had mixed feelings as the event concluded.

'Those fellas had spent so much time over in the corner playing poker that they never really did get over to the craps and 21 tables. Most of them, as I recall, even stayed on about a week after the little ol' convention was officially over.'

"Jack Binion asked Vickrey a year later if he was interested in holding the same get-together again. Vickrey said thanks, but he thought he might try some other promotions. In 1970 the Binions launched the World Series of Poker at the Horseshoe where, over the next decade or so, it was to gain widely recognized status as the biggest pure gambling event in Nevada and one of the very largest in the world."

The entire 1970 event took place in one small room, currently the baccarat alcove. Five games were played and the 63-year-old Moss won them all. He received a small trophy and whatever money he had earned at the table. In a classic photograph taken of the Texas gamblers who attended the event, about 30 men are gathered around a poker table with some trophies sitting on it. The trophies were awarded by the men to each other. (See photo on page 17.)

"In those days it warn't no one game an' it warn't no freeze-out," Johnny Moss related. "You had to win all the games, win all the money. Then you're the best player, an' they vote on you. It was pretty nice, you know, because there were a lot of good players in town. But most good players are only good at one game, an' I was good at 'em all. I win all five games that year an' they give me a big trophy. In '74 they give me this here gold bracelet with the date engraved on the back. I win a silver cup, too—solid silver, engraved. In all, it must have weighed 40 pounds."

The idea for the WSOP probably had been germinating in Benny Binion's mind since 1949, the year that he set up the famous heads-up game between Nick "The Greek" Dandalos, 57, and Johnny Moss, 42. Al Alvarez described the game in his best-seller, *The Biggest Game in Town*. "Binion had a shrewd eye for free publicity for his recently acquired casino. Even before the first break, the table, which Benny had thoughtfully positioned near the entrance to the casino, was surrounded by crowds six deep, drawn by rumors of the biggest game the town had ever seen."

The game lasted for five months with breaks for sleep every four or five days, "although The Greek spent most of his nonpoker time at the craps tables. They began by playing five-card stud and switched to draw, seven-card stud, seven-card stud high-low, ace-to-five lowball and deuce-to-seven lowball. Wealthy aspirants were permitted to change in to the game for a minimum of $10,000, but none lasted more than a day or two."

The tall, trim Dandalos, who had a degree from an English university, was reputed to have broken all the gamblers on the East coast, including the legendary Arnold Rothstein, winning $60 million in the process, most of which he lost on the horses or craps. Moss, who (like Benny Binion) had a second grade education, was a Texas road gambler who played during the East Texas oil boom and the Depression. He also played golf for big sums of money, as much as $100,000 a round, often for $1,000 a hole. Dandalos died broke on Christmas day in 1966. Binion died a millionaire on Christmas day in 1989. Moss died a champion in December 1995.

To gain a better perspective on the Las Vegas poker scene in 1970, note these statistics published in the 1985 WSOP brochure: "In 1970 there were only 70 licensed poker tables in Nevada casinos. They produced $5.2 million in revenue for the state. In Clark County (Las Vegas) during the same year, there were 47 tables on which there was $4.5 million in state revenue that was reflected in the table rake." Binion's Horseshoe did not have a poker room at the time. It was not until 1988, when it acquired the Mint, that the Horseshoe had enough space to open its own card room.

Further statistics from the 1985 brochure document the growth of poker in Nevada casinos over the next 10 years: "In 1980 there were 423 poker tables at Nevada casinos producing revenue for the state of $50,164,000. Far more than half of these were still in the Las Vegas or Clark County area where there were 297 tables that had brought in $39,693,000."

The growth of poker nationwide often is credited to the growth of the World Series of Poker under the leadership of Jack Binion.

The 1970 World Series of Poker. Standing (l to r): Jack Straus, Benny Binion, J.R. Green, John Luke, Don Howard, Joe Floyd and Bob Hooks. Seated (l to r): George Barnes, Curtis Skinner, Johnny Moss, Chill Wills, Titanic Thompson, Joe Bernstein, Puggy Pearson and Jimmy Casella.

# 1971 World Championship Event
## 2nd World Series of Poker
Number of Entries: 6

─────── The Championship Table ───────

| The Finalists | Hometown |
|---|---|
| Johnny Moss | Odessa, TX |
| Puggy Pearson | Nashville, TN |
| Sailor Roberts | San Angelo, TX |
| Jack Straus | Fort Worth, TX |
| Doyle Brunson | Lubbock, TX |
| Jimmy Casella | Texas |

Most of the road gamblers traveled to the early Series mainly to play in the high-stakes side games, as well as enter a tournament or two. This is why you see the names of so many old road gamblers on the winners' list of the World Series of Poker in the '70s and early '80s. It wasn't until around 1983 when satellites came into existence that you started seeing players win events at the Series who hadn't traveled the Southern poker circuit or played in the big games in Texas and Louisiana.

The WSOP format was changed in 1971 when the championship was determined by process of elimination. According to the 1983 WSOP brochure:

It was most fitting that Johnny Moss was the first to win the title in the new show-down style competition.

It was not long before the idea suggested itself that a full-scale poker tournament would not only attract the world's best poker buffs, but would quickly develop into a major media event. It was thought that poker had thus far failed to capture press attention because it did not have a series of competitions, as did the other sports, culminating in one grand play-off. In other words, what the game needed was a real tournament where the best players could meet to match wits and skills to determine who among their ranks qualified to bear the world championship title.

| The Finish | Prize Money |
|------------|-------------|
| Moss | $30,000 |
| Pearson | -0- |

"No-limit hold'em was first scheduled as the championship event in 1971," the brochure continued. "This variety of poker originated in Texas and was selected as the appropriate form of the game for determing the title winner because it draws on all the poker skills, especially bluffing."

Of course no-limit hold'em also was the game of choice for most of the road gamblers who comprised the vast majority of the players in the early World Series tournaments. The buy-in for the 1971 event was $5,000. In 1972 it rose to $10,000 and has remained the same for thirty years.

"We didn't have any idea of it getting big," Jack Binion said about the World Series. "But there was a kid on television here (in Las Vegas) who moved to a station in Los Angeles and got that station to cover it. By 1972 we were on national TV. That was the year that Amarillo Slim won it. He wasn't even considered one of the very top players until then. But he got himself on Johnny Carson, worked hard getting publicity, and now he's a household word anywhere. And the tournament has just kept growing."

"Anybody can lift their chips up and down, but they can't always push 'em in the pot. That's goin' down a different street. You gotta be cold about that, real cold."

— Johnny Moss to Jon Bradshaw in 1973

"I won't let Johnny play poker at all in the house. They just get so nasty when they're playin', droppin' cigarette butts on the rugs and ever'thing."

— Virgie Moss to reporter Al Reinert at the 1973 WSOP

# 1972 World Championship Event
## 3rd World Series of Poker
### Number of Entries: 8

————— The Championship Table —————

| The Finalists | Hometown |
|---|---|
| Johnny Moss | Odessa, TX |
| Puggy Pearson | Nashville, TN |
| Sailor Roberts | San Angelo, TX |
| Jack Straus | Fort Worth, TX |
| Amarillo Slim Preston | Amarillo, TX |
| Doyle Brunson | Lubbock, TX |

Amarillo Slim's victory at the 1972 World Series of Poker triggered an avalanche of national media attention, primarily because the tall toothpick from Texas is a natural-born promoter. The 2002 Binion's Horseshoe web site described Preston's impact:

> In 1972 when Thomas 'Amarillo Slim' Preston won the title and went on the talk-show circuit, the WSOP began to gain a wider following. A year later Benny Binion participated in the Oral History Project at the University of Nevada-Reno and discussed the World Series with interviewer Mary Ellen Glass. 'We had eight players last year, and this year we had 13,' he said. "I look to have better than 20 next year. It's even liable to get up to be 50, might get up to be more than that. It will eventually."

Binion's prophecy turned out to be modest. Nine years later in 1982, the championship event drew 104 entrants. Five years after that there were 2,141 participants in the WSOP. The 2002 WSOP attracted 7,595 entries. Whereas only 12 events, mostly hold'em and seven-card stud, were scheduled as recently as 1988, the 2002 tournament offered 37 tournaments in a wide variety of games.

| The Finish | Prize Money |
|------------|-------------|
| 1st Preston | $80,000 |
| 2nd Pearson | -0- |

Amarillo Slim made eleven appearances on Johnny Carson's *Tonight Show*, and had three stints on *60 Minutes*. As a result he became the spokesman for modern poker, the icon of the poker world. With his gift for gab and colorful stories, he was much better in front of a camera than Johnny Moss. Credited with helping bring poker out of the smoky back rooms of the past and into the living rooms of the general public, Preston influenced the popularity and growth of the WSOP with magnum force. He also wrote a hastily put-together book titled *Maverick Poker*, of which he is not extremely proud, although it further publicized the game of poker in a positive way.

## Highlights
In 1972 the buy-in for the no-limit hold'em tournament was increased from $5,000 to $10,000. In addition to the no-limit hold'em championship event, a five-card stud tournament was added to the WSOP schedule at the players' request. Legendary stud player Bill Boyd won the event.

"Hey, Greek, I'm the world champeen at this here game. How come you're only makin' me eight-to-one? Ain't you read my book? It says right on the cover, Amarillo Slim shows you how he beats 'em all. Hell, I'd get better odds in a spelling bee." — Amarillo Slim to oddsmaker Jimmy "The Greek" Snyder at the 1973 WSOP

"That Slim, he always had a lot of country con. That book of his is a joke. He may have won last year, but he was lucky. He's good, but he ain't great."
— Johnny Moss to Jon Bradshaw at the 1973 WSOP

# Thomas "Amarillo Slim" Preston
## Slim 'n Benny: The Old Days at the World Series
### Interview with a Champ (1999) by Dana Smith

Amarillo Slim Preston—no matter how large the crowd, it's hard not to notice a man with so distinctive an appearance. Maybe it's his custom made ostrich boots, the ones with the spades, diamonds, hearts, clubs and his name engraved on them—"I've got these in fourteen different colors, brought nine pairs here with me. No wonder they had to send a limousine for me." Or the gold buttons on his Western shirt—"I wear uncirculated $1.00 gold pieces over the buttons on my shirts (Benny wore them too) and matching cuff links with $5.00 pieces." Or just the total persona of a gambler who has helped more than any other to bring respectability to poker —"I've gone out and done some things that nobody else has."

Slim and I escaped the crowd in the poker room during the '99 World Series of Poker for an intimate conversation in the midst of a few hundred of our closest friends in the sportsbook at the Horseshoe where the fast-talkin' Texas toothpick, the most famous poker player in the world, rolled out a string of stories like a kitten playfully unraveling a ball of twine. First there were the Benny Binion tales, then the Betty Carey episode followed by the infamous "I'll slit my throat if a woman ever . . ." misquote. Enough verbiage to choke a horse, as Slim himself might say.

"The ol' man willed me his horse when he died," the colorful story teller reminisced." I have his personal horse at my ranch right now—why, I knew Benny Binion better than anybody alive. I met him when I was a kid in Texas, back when I thought that I was just being mischievous, but the government thought that I was bein' a little more than that. I was a little rowdy and Benny liked that. And he could trust me. I wasn't *this* big around, but I wouldn't give a grizzly bear the road."

*Did you and Benny play poker or do business together?*

I never played poker with him in my life, but he played my hand for me one day at the Horseshoe. "Lemme sit down here," he says. I said okay and just walked off. When I came back, a crowd had gathered around and I thought, "What in the hell, I guess the ol' man's pissed off all my chips." Right about then somebody bet and he just moved in on 'em. After the guy threw his hand away, Benny says to me, "Look at my hand, see what I got."

"What do you mean?" I asked.

"Well, I didn't have my glasses on and I couldn't see my hand, but I didn't want nobody to know it." That ol' sonnagun bet all my money and didn't even know what he had!

*What then?*

I was doin' a lot of TV after the World Series first started, so I'm in Arkansas, buying some registered Hereford cattle from the Rockefeller Corporation. I was gonna artificially inseminate them. Them poor ol' cows get milked twice a day and only get to mate once a year—just seems like they deserve a better fate than that. Anyway, I'd done the Johnny Carson show three or four times by then, and Tom Snyder and I had gotten to be friends—he had the Tomorrow Show right after Carson's Tonight Show. So Snyder's show coordinator runs me down back there in Arkansas saying, "Slim, we want you to come do the show on a certain date because Bob Hope's gonna be on then and he makes Snyder nervous and we know that you'll relax him."

"I'll come on the condition that I can bring my own guest," I said. "Well, we don't do that," he answered.

"Suits me," I said and hung up the phone. So the next time they called, it was Snyder himself on the phone.

"Slim, who would you bring?" he asks.

"I'd bring Benny Binion," I said.

"Sure you will!" he answered. You see, the whole world couldn't get Benny to do a TV show because he didn't want no publicity. "But if I bring him," I said, "you'll have to give us the whole show."

"Okay, but bring one other guest, too," he answered.

So I brought Benny and Joe Bernstein, the gambler, on the show with me and we put on an hour's commercial for the Horseshoe. Me 'n Benny had made up a signal so that if they asked him something and he was in a jam to answer it, I could take him off the hook. So, somebody asks him, "Benny, why is it that those places out there on the Strip in Vegas have a $500 limit and you've got no limit?" I thought, "Oh, how's Benny gonna handle that one?"

"Well, they got great big hotels and little bitty bankrolls," he said. "I got a little bitty hotel and a great big bankroll." It went over good. About a minute later somebody asked, "But Mr. Binion, aren't you afraid that somebody will break the bank?"

"Well, not really," he said. "I've got a damned good head start on 'em."

*But there's more to this story, right?*

Yeah, we took a limo down to Rodeo Drive to have us some suits made. "Slim, tell the driver to turn around and let's go back over there to get Joe to make up a couple of Western tuxedos," Benny says. So I tell the driver to turn around and he answers, "OK, but I've gotta go down here and turn off and do so and so." The ol' man repeats again, "Tell him he needs to turn around now." He said he couldn't.

"Ralph, you really do need to turn around," I insist and finally he did. We were about to get pinched and the ol' man knew it. Benny was tough, but a lot of people don't realize that he was a good-hearted, generous man. He was either the gentlest bad guy or the baddest good guy you'd ever seen. And that's a pretty good epitaph for him.

*A story goes around that happened years ago about a remark you made to a woman at the World Series of Poker.*

This is the factual account. It used to be that we took very few breaks, we played till it was over, but that was before the media got a hold of it. In about the first two or three hours of the tournament, a lady named Vera who wasn't a very popular person got hold of this many checks. Then we took a break and went into the Sombrero Room where the Associated Press and a bunch of people were yakking with me. So here comes this big woman, Vera, whose family owned some big ol' cosmetics company, about 1,500 stores. She busts right in, but that was okay with me, it didn't matter. "Mr. Slim," she says (she called me Mr. Slim because she was trying to show me some respect in front of the media), "what do you think about a lady getting a hold of that many chips?"

"I think it's great," I answer.

"Well, it's a certainty that I'm gonna win this World Series," she blurts out.

"Vera, if you win the World Series of Poker you can take a dull knife and cut my throat!" That's exactly what I said—and I meant it.

"What will you lay to one that I don't win it?"she asks.

Before I could speak up, Frank Gish was standing there and he says, "I'll lay you 40-to-1." I was gonna lay her 200-to-1, but she took Frank's offer for a little bit of money.

Later I was quoted as saying, "If a woman ever wins the World Series, I'll cut my throat." I didn't say that, but I caught a lot of heat from the gals, the lesser lady players, although when I told the good ones how it was, they knew Vera and understood what I meant by my remark. To this day, I'm still quoted incorrectly.

*You know the great lady player Betty Carey quite well ...*

Yes, she's back in Wyoming, has a little girl child, and is completely away from gaming.

*What about the big poker games you played with her?*

Betty is the best woman poker player that I've ever seen. Jimmy Chagra bankrolled her with $100,000 to play me head-up out at the Hilton the first time she played me, but I had a tell on Betty and I beat her. You see, I got her to talking to me the first time we played and I knew her hand—believe me, I knew her hand. That's why a lot of people won't talk to me when I'm playing—they betray themselves. I had heard Betty say that something she was drinking tasted real good, so I knew how she sounded when she was sincere. Then this pot came up—it was so big that a show dog couldn't jump over it—and I asked her, "How do you like your hand, Betty?" And she says, "Boy, this is a real good hand." But it didn't sound the same as before—I knew she was lyin'. So I called her and sure 'nough, she didn't have anything.

Now in her defense, a broker from New York staked Betty to play me $100,000 here at the Horseshoe and I beat her the first game. When we got through she said, "We might play again." So I gave her a $100 bill to call her backer so that I could find out where she was getting that money. Not all trappers wear fur caps, you know. Then people woke up to what I was doin', how I got a tell on her, and they told her not to talk to me, that no matter what I said she wasn't to answer me. So, the fourth time we played she came to the table with things in her ears.

"I'm ready to play another freezeout," she says.

"Betty, we're playing Texas rules this time," I answer. "When you lose one, you must bet two, that's the way the Texans do." You follow? So she leaves and comes back with $200,000 to play me. And she broke me in about eight minutes.

I had won the first two matches that we played at the Hilton, plus the first one that we played at Binion's, but on the last one I got loser because I made her bet two "the way the Texans do." You see, I knew who her backer was and I wanted to scratch him up a little, win something with whiskers on it you know.

*Has the World Series changed a lot since the old days?*

The Series or the property? The property has changed a lot, but the Series is so big and so successful that you could hold it at Pahrump out there in the hole where Teddy (Binion) had his silver buried and people would show up. 'Course, Benny used to serve only premier food, too, but all I know is that I miss him, and not just here at the Horseshoe.

He was at my ranch one time while a buyer from a big stud farm was there looking at a mare that I had. The buyer offered me about three times what she was worth.

"You oughta pick out something else," I said, "I don't want to sell that mare," so I sent some of my guys with him to look over some of my yearlings. "If you find something there that you want, fine, but this mare you can't have."

Then Benny gets to walking around and looking at that filly and he says, "You know, Slim, she reminds me of the best son-nabitch I ever owned."

And I'm thinking oh, my gawd, he's putting the touch on me, so I say, "Yeah, but she's not much 'count."

"Yeah she is," he says. Later we're riding down the road in my car, he's staying at my home, and he says, "What do you want fer her?" He always said "fer."

"I don't want nothing fer her. You know what I turned down."

"Well, I'll stand to get robbed a little bit. What do you want fer her?"

"Nothing. She's not for sale!"

So he squirreled up like an ol' toad, wouldn't hardly talk to me. About three weeks later I sent one of my rigs up to Montana to Benny's ranch with a paint llama, a gray mule that Rex Cabo had wanted (he's a big boss in Texas and was a friend of ours), and that mare that Benny wanted—her name was Miss Flaming Becky. I gave them all to him. That llama was a spotted paint, unusual, that I had brought in from Argentina.

*What an extraordinary thing to do.*

We don't do ordinary things, hon. Benny didn't call to thank me, didn't acknowledge that he'd gotten them, didn't do a damned thing. So I'm out here in Vegas and I'm up early one morning and Benny calls me—me and him, we'd get up early and go out to get a shave and then we'd eat strawberries, we were both sucker for fresh strawberries. "What you gonna do this afternoon?" he asks.

"Nothin'," I say.

"Let's go to a sale. Wayne Newton's having a big one out at his ranch."

"Benny, I don't own any Arabians (and he didn't either) and I can rope and drag every sonnabitch Arabian I've ever seen faster than he can run." But we go to the sale anyway. Turns out that they had a longhorn cattle sale, too, and damned if the ol' man didn't get to biddin' and buyin' and biddin' and buyin' and he bought two or three truckloads of them registered longhorn cows and calves and some heifers.

About ten days later I'm back home and my foreman calls me saying, "Slim, what do you want to do with these longhorn pairs that's down here in this truck?"

"Whose truck is it?" I ask.

"Well, it's got a T. J. on it (Teddy Jane)."

"Oh, that's some of Benny's stock. Just put 'em in a lot and feed and water them, they probably want to rest them because they're going to Fort Worth or somewhere." So a while later, the foreman calls me back and says, "They're to stay here."

I don't even snap, you understand, I just pick up the phone and call Benny.

"What the hell do you want me to do with these long-horns?"

"Oh," he says, "they're yours."

"Okay," I say, never saying thank you or nothing. He had sent me twelve registered longhorn pairs, meaning a cow and a calf. The cows were sucking a big calf and they were heavy springers that probably were six months pregnant with another one. That was the reciprocation that Benny made for my mare. And not one word was ever said.

*Do you enjoy the World Series as much as you used to?*

I enjoy the camaraderie, the how are you and how've you been, and do you remember the wa-wa-wa, and how are your cutting horses, all that. Then I sit down to play and visit with everyone and in ten minutes I feel like I'm in the electric chair—I'd rather be anywhere else in the world. How can I say it? I'm pokered out. I must've done something right along the way, though, because I have a lot of friends.

The only thing that has excited me in my life during the last 15 years is that about three months ago, I was told that I was one of only two unanimous inductees into the Legends of Nevada at the Tropicana Hotel and Casino. Benny Binion and Howard Hughes and I were all inducted, and only two of us were unanimous. Now that makes a country sonnagun feel good, you know what I'm sayin'? I got all dressed up and then a big screen 'bout as big as Boulder Dam came on at both ends of the showroom and a senator

Amarillo Slim Preston at the 1974 World Series of Poker.

from Washington lied and told what a good sonnagun I am and the governor and all the prominent people said I was as fine a man as ever put powder in a safe—no, they didn't say that, I'm just kiddin,' hon. And they played my song: "Do you dare make a bet with Amarillo Slim? You play his game with one condition for him. From greens on the golf to baskets in the gym, do you dare make a bet with Amarillo Slim? Hell, the devil don't bet with Amarillo Slim." Everybody in the casino stood when they played it and that made me feel good, hon.

*You wrote a book about poker years ago.*

Yeah, and you can't get it nowadays. The original title was "Amarillo Slim in a World of Fat People," but some clever guy changed the title to *Maverick Poker*. There's nothing in it worth a damn, but there were 29 authors at the author's convention in Los Angels the next year—Norman Mailer had just done Marilyn and Jonathan Livingston Seagull (I called it "The Birds") was just out—and I got all the limelight. You know what reverse psychology is? I came out from behind my table and gave out books and told all the press guys in my line, "Why don't you get out of this line and go over there in that best-seller's line so you can get yourself something fit to read? My book isn't worth nine-cents and eggs." Now guess what that caused? The people that were in the other lines came over and got in mine!

*You're good with the press and that's one reason why you've helped bring poker into the national spotlight.*

Yeah, you hear that a lot. I went out and did some things that nobody else did. I've done three specials for 60 Minutes on Sunday nights, and hell, I've been on the Carson show eleven times.

When I first meet a guy and he asks me what I do, I generally say, "I'm a gambler," because I want to see his reaction. I want to know if he thinks that a gambler is someone who just crawled out from under a rock or hustles bribes or deals in narcotics. I don't do any of those things. I'm a gambler but I've been accepted. You know what that means? I've spoken twice at the National Press Club in Washington, D. C., and that's reserved for foreign and national dignitaries. I've even addressed the United States Senate—and I'm a gambler, you understand? You shoulda heard the questions they asked me: One big-shot senator asked me something and I answered, "Well, sir, I really and truly don't think that's any of your business," and the room broke up. No one else would talk to him that way, but I got away with it.

*Do you stake a lot of guys in poker?*

No ma'am. I help some guys but I don't stake a lot of guys. Here's why: Turn it around and you could never arrange a scenario when I would ask them to stake me. If I was cold broke and destitute, I wouldn't ask anyone around here to stake me, so I'd feel like a fool if I staked one of them. I never did lend anybody $20,000 that I didn't get paid—and I never did lend anybody $200 and get it back. Now that tells you something: He's a $200 sonnagun to start with if that's all he asks you for.

*What are doing these days, Slim?*

Nothin'. I'm the same as always, the same everyday. I don't play that much poker anymore, hardly play at all. I'm building some golf courses and go quail hunting nearly every day. And I go to all the sporting events, the Masters golf tournament, the World Series of Poker, the Super Bowl of football, the National Finals Rodeo, go to Europe three or four times a year, get a six-pak of young blondes and cabaret once in a while. I'm not being boastful, just tellin' you what I do with my time. I don't think I'm pretentious about anything. My wife and I are very fond of and protective toward our three children. We have six little filly grandbabies and one little boy grandchild, and they are our life. We have a 6,800 square-foot home, looks like a hotel—I have my own golf course in my back yard, a professional tennis court, a king-sized swimming pool. I'm 70 years old now and I'm at peace with me and you and my Maker, the whole world, you know what I mean? And I don't take this gaming as seriously as most people.

*So, in addition to your lifestyle, your personal values have remained the same for years.*

Yes. Mike Sexton says to me the other day, "Slim I have your phone number, it's been the same forever, but what's your mailing address?" I answer, "Mike, all you've gotta do is send it to Amarillo Slim, Amarillo, Texas, and I'll get it." No one in the world believes that, but it's true. Somebody called the long distance operator at area code 806 and asked for the phone number of Amarillo Slim—and the operator gave it to him. As well as I love life, that's the truth! In my hometown, I'm known. Amarillo's a good town and the population has been the same for the past 30 years, never varies—every time some woman gets pregnant, some man leaves town.

*You're bad, Slim!*

I don't mean nothin' when I talk bad, okay, hon?

*I understand, Slim. After all, I read your book, you know.*

"Some of these guys are real uptight. It's so quiet you could hear an ant pee on cotton." — Amarillo Slim Preston

"It'd be like us takin ' in each other's wash fer a livin'." — Amarillo Slim to reporter Al Reinert in 1973 on why the top players don't play against each other in cash games

1972 Champion Amarillo Slim Preston, 1970-71-74 Champion Johnny Moss, and World Series of Poker founder Benny Binion at the 1974 World Series of Poker at Binion's Horseshoe Casino.

# 1973 World Championship Event
## 4th World Series of Poker
Number of Entries: 13

─────── ## The Championship Table ───────

| The Finalists | Hometown |
|---|---|
| Bobby Brazil | Lake Tahoe, NV |
| Bob Hooks | Edgewood,TX |
| Johnny Moss | Odessa, TX |
| Puggy Pearson | Las Vegas, NV |
| Sailor Roberts | San Angelo, TX |
| Jack Straus | Fort Worth, TX |

─────── ## The Last Hand ───────

**Pearson's Cards**     **Moss' Cards**

_____ **Flop** _____**Turn** _____ **River**

| The Finish | Prize Money |
|---|---|
| 1st Pearson | $130,000 |
| 2nd Moss | -0- |

## How It Happened

Moss pushed in his last $40,000 on the flop with K-J offsuit. When the board came with a Q-10, it gave Moss an open-end straight draw. With the nut flush draw and one overcard, Pearson called the bet with A-7 suited and he and Moss laid their cards open on the felt. Pearson didn't make the flush, but he still won the hand with an ace high.

## Highlights

1973 was the first championship event to be video taped. It was narrated by legendary oddsmaker Jimmy "The Greek" Snyder and, in the opinion of many World Series aficionados, is the most entertaining WSOP video ever filmed. It was a winner-take-all tournament, so the 45-year-old Pearson won the entire $130,000. They played until 3:00 a.m. on the first day and resumed late the next afternoon. "I learnt to play with gamblers!" Pearson exclaimed at the end of the event, which took 19 hours to play. Jon Bradshaw chronicled the final table action in his 1975 book *Fast Company*, which includes colorful interviews with Moss and Pearson.

Reporter Al Reinert (*Texas Monthly*) also covered the '73 Series and described Pearson: "Pug looks like he's between acts as a circus clown, but he's one of the best three all-around card players alive." Reinert wrote a vivid portrayal of Moss: "Johnny Moss' face is transparently blank, the practiced result of 50 years of self-induced rigor mortis." According to Reinert, Moss had lost "an easy quarter million" in the month prior to the WSOP in the big games at the Aladdin.

During the early Series, players were allowed to buy insurance on their hands, side bets based on the probability of one hand winning over another designed to cover a player's possible losses. In one hand against Straus, Moss wanted 2-to-1 insurance, but Jack

Binion offered him only 3-to-2. Moss passed on the wager, but won the hand and knocked Straus out in third place. Snyder had picked Straus as the favorite to win the tournament at 9-to-2. Amarillo Slim Preston, who was knocked out next to last, was hawking his new book, *Maverick Poker*, at the Series, stating its price as "six ninety-five or fifty dollars fer an autograph't one."

In addition to the championship tournament, four preliminary tournaments were played. Pearson won two of them, seven-card stud and no-limit hold'em. Aubrey Day and Jack Straus were declared co-winners of the deuce-to-seven draw event, and Sam Angel won the seven-card razz tournament. Seven thousand articles about the WSOP were published in newspapers and magazines in 1973. The next WSOP video tape came in 1978.

# Walter Clyde "Puggy" Pearson
## On the Road Again
### Interview with a Champ (1996) by Dana Smith

Remember the hippy vans of the '60s painted bumper to bumper in psychedelic colors? I saw one at the World Series of Poker that was far more sophisticated, bigger, better, more befitting the legendary poker player who had it custom painted to herald his arrival during his anticipated odyssey to visit cardrooms across the nation. *Card Player* publisher Linda Johnson and I talked with the owner of this "little house on the poker prairie" about his colorful background, his distinguished accomplishments, a few of his legendary exploits, and his plans to explore new horizons in his chosen profession.

Puggy Pearson, Poker Hall of Famer and 1973 *WSOP* champion, held court in his imperial digs, a 38-foot long, diesel-powered Imperial Holiday Rambler parked outside the entrance to the poker room at Binion's Horseshoe. We lounged comfortably in the motorhome's spacious living room, made wider by its "pop-out" feature, from which we could look down the Chinese carpeted hallway to the bedroom just past the dining nook, bathroom, laundry area, and full kitchen. The TV, VCR, and CB were mounted near the driver's panel.

Professionally painted in neon colors across the outside of the huge rolling domicile are a royal flush, pool cue, and Pearson's famous saying, "I'll play any man from any land any game that he can name for any amount that I count," with the disclaimer "providing I like it" tacked onto the end of the sentence in insurance-policy-size type. His colorful, homespun and genteel lingo rang a reminiscent bell from my childhood in the deep South as Pearson explained to me his motivation for buying the $200,000 rig and the dream that he hopes to see come true with it.

"During my first hitch in the Navy (I did three of them), when I was 17 years old, I was in China," he said. "My ambition then was to get me a 16-cylinder Cadillac, put my pool cue and everything in it, and tour the country because I love to hustle. Of course, evolution took care of that—and destitution and women—and I wound up with my nose to the grindstone under these poker tables."

*So you've been working hard all these years?*

I've been working awful hard. As a matter of fact, I think that poker players work harder than people who work nine-to-five.

*What about this dream of yours with your motorhome?*

It's the epitome of all scufflers' dreams: to be able to set sail with an 800-number, and match up with anybody in the country, don't make no difference who they are. I think I'll get all the notoriety in the world, I'll make the front page of every little town, and I think I'll have more business than I know what to do with.

*What type of business?*

I intend to set it up so that I can play something like a $10,000 freezeout, a $50,000 freezeout, or even a $1 million freezeout providing they put up the money. I won't ever play for over three hours. And it'll be big for the joints because if they publicize my arrival in advance, it'll draw all kinds of people from all over everywhere to see me perform. I'll also be able to solicit the best players in the world into the casino. It could be a win-win-win for everybody, the casinos, the players and me. You see what I'm saying?

I'm gonna' try to tour the entire country starting right after the WSOP, and then I might just ship the rig to Europe. I'll be pulling up in front of all the major casinos, I'll have me a P.A. system, and when I turn it on, I'll sing 'em a little song called "The Roving Gambler." You know how that goes?

*I'd love to hear it.*

"I'm a roving gambler, I ramble all around. Wherever I meet with a deck of cards, I'll lay my money down. I've gambled all down in Texas, I've gambled up in Maine. And now I'm gonna' do it all over again."

*So you like center stage?*

Oh, I love it! I'm just a ham and that's all there is to it. I'm a top-notch entertainer. When you're playing poker, there are eight or nine guys around the table and I like to keep the floor. I want to keep the focus on me.

*What will be your first stop?*

Tennessee, which I call "Al Gore country." My people are all from Tennessee, and my daughter's with a big law firm there. Back in Nashville, I'm Daniel Boone, Davey Crocket, and Jim Bowie all rolled up into one: I'm the "Ayatolla of Tennessee." In fact, when they first started calling me the "ayatolla," I didn't know that it was a religious title; I just thought that it meant "the boss." And that kinda' appealed to me.

*How did you get started playing poker?*

Well, you know that I used to be one of the top ten pool players in the world, but I started playing poker when I was in New Guinea in the Navy. I'm laying on about the third bunk up and I'm looking down at the floor where they're playing stud poker. This guy's got a queen in the hole and he hits the deck kinda' funny and there's a queen laying on the bottom of it. Well, when the smoke cleared, he wound up winning with two queens. So I thought that maybe this was a game that I'd like to play, too.

*What about your life before the Navy?*

I come from a large family, eight brothers and sisters. Momma and Daddy were both illiterate and we were poor. Every time the rent came due, we had to move. From the time I was 10 until I went into the Navy at age 17, I lived in 19 different places between Nashville and the countryside. I used to take biscuits with thick gravy on them to school for lunch; everybody else had meat on their sandwiches. I'd never seen a loaf of bread until we moved to Nashville when I was 10 years old. When I went to the filling station with another little boy and he gave me the ends of the loaf, I thought I was getting a piece of cake.

*How did you get your nickname?*

When I was about 12 years old, I was very athletic. They'd just built the framework to a Nazarene church about a block away from my house. And so now I'm on the framework walking on my hands across these 2x4s, showing off for a cute little gal. (There's always been a gal in my life and that's caused me all of my problems.) I missed one of the boards and fell, and I came right down on my nose. There's nothing in the world worse for a teenaged kid than having his features displaced. You project yourself into your environment and people absorb you as to the way you look. Once your features get displaced, people automatically look at you differently. The kids started calling me "No Nose" or "Flat Face." Then around the poolrooms, it got to be "Pug."

*What's the biggest score you've ever made?*

I've probably lost bigger scores than I've made. But I've made a lot of big scores of $300,000 to $500,000. That was big, big money back in those days. I used to go over to the Dunes and lose $60,000 or $70,000, and then I'd take the difference in that amount and $100,000 and go over to the crap table and try to get it back and then I'd end up losing the whole wad.

You know, there's only three basic things to being a good outside scuffler—knowing when you've got the best of it; money management; and managing yourself. That third thing is the hardest part. If you can handle those three departments, you're gonna end up in the plus column. What busts all would-be scufflers and gamblers is the steam factor.

Back in the old days I got broke forty times a year. Then I'd go get money from somebody. I had lots of stamina; I could stay up for a week at a time. I'd bounce back up and get in the big money again. And then I'd get broke again. That's the way it is with the typical gambler.

*What's the truth to the story about the dealer hitting you over the head with her high heels?*

Well, that's a true story that happened at the Dunes years ago. Something happened and well, you know how I am: I threw the cards or did something like I always do. The dealer didn't say nothing, she just kept on dealing. But when she got through, she picked up a double handful of my black chips and threw them all over the casino. Johnny Moss was the poker room boss at that time, and we were crawlin' around on the floor trying to find all them chips. "What would you do if somebody did you that way?" I asked him, but I can't repeat his answer. The next thing I know, one of them big ol' dealers came over and I fell backward over a chair. While he had me down, the lady dealer started beating me on the head with her high heels. Every time I've ever gotten into a fight or scuffle, I've always gotten the worst of it. Nobody ever wins in a fight, anyway.

*So what's the real Puggy like?*

You wanna' know the honest-to-God truth? He's a little bitty, lovable pussycat. I remember back when I was a paperboy and I'd go to these yards to leave the paper, and there would be some ol' dog that would come runnin' out to the fence. He's gonna' just eat you up. Well, you'd open the gate and he'd just run up under the porch. And that's about the way I am.

*Have you enjoyed your life?*

Well, I surely have. I've had my good times and my bad times, like everybody else. I've always said that life is 98 percent luck and about a half of a percent skill. As you go down the road of life, you've always got more than one way to go: You can go to the right or you can go to the left. If you go to the right and you screw up, then you always wonder what the heck would've happened if you'd gone the other way. When people get old, they think about the past, about the mistakes they've made. I've enjoyed my life, yes; but I've always wanted to be of benefit to my fellow man, and I feel like I haven't been as such, like I could've been. To me, the people who control all of the money in the world are *not* the smartest people—he smartest ones are the people that make computers, the people that go to the moon. They contribute a lot more to the world than the money controllers. I would have liked to have contributed more to mankind than I have.

*How could you have done that?*

Well, I couldn't have because destiny didn't make it that way. I never had a chance to get an education past the eighth grade, and that's about the equivalent of a third grade education these days.

*What do you think will happen if poker tournaments and players begin to get sponsorship?*

I don't think that poker has been handled properly so far. You see, poker needs stars like Jack Nicklaus and Arnold Palmer are in the golf world. They're spokesmen, and people like to hear them. Gambling has come so far so fast in the last few years, even though it's still frowned upon by most religions. (Of course, the biggest gamblers in the world are the people that play the stock market.) If poker is to go further, we need personalities, spokesmen for our profession. I feel like I'm in the best position of anybody right now to be that kind of a person for the card players and the scufflers of the world.

"A gambler's ace is his ability to think clearly under stress. That's very important because, you see, fear is the basis of all mankind. In cards you psych 'em out, you shark 'em, you put the fear of God in 'em. That's life." —Puggy Pearson

# 1974 World Championship Event
## 5th World Series of Poker
### Number of Entries: 16

—————— The Championship Table ——————

| The Finalists | Hometown |
|---|---|
| Johnny Moss | Odessa, TX |
| Crandall Addington | San Antonio, TX |

Other players included Doyle Brunson, Puggy Pearson, Sailor Roberts, Bob Hooks, Jimmy Casella and Amarillo Slim Preston.

## Johnny Moss (1907-1995)

"Johnny's passing is the end of an era," Jim Albrecht, longtime director of the World Series of Poker said. "He was the link between the Old West school of gambling and the modern days of a forty-page rule book. Ask all the living legends, they'll credit Johnny Moss with being the last of the great road gamblers. He was the Master."

Moss was the son of poor itinerants who moved to Fort Worth in a covered wagon when he was a year old. His mother died the next year and his father moved Moss and his older brother and sister to Dallas, where he sold the wagon to the fire department and settled the family in a three-room "shotgun" house. "You could open the front door and shoot right through the place," Moss said.

When his father became disabled, Moss quit school and began selling newspapers to help support the family. He was eight years old. "Benny Binion and Chill Wills, we was all gamblin' on the streets of East Dallas when we was kids," he told Jon Bradshaw, author of *Fast Company*. "I really learnt gamblin' as a newsboy—shootin' dice in the alley and sellin' newspapers in the domino halls, the men there learnt me how to play real well." As a teenager he worked as a lookout for a Dallas gambling house whose owner taught him how to play draw poker. Moss learned to play hold'em at the Elks Club in a $2-limit game, earning his buy-ins at the domino parlors. For Moss, gambling was a way out of poverty.

| The Finish | Prize Money |
|---|---|
| 1st Moss | $160,000 |
| 2nd Addington | -0- |

When he was 19 years old, Moss became a road gambler, taking his bride of one year, Virgie Ann, along with him to keep an eye on the money. She remained by his side for the next 70 years, in their home in Odessa and later in Las Vegas. "I don't have much regard for money," he told Bradshaw. "Money's just paper to gamble with. But Virgie, well, Virgie's a millionaire."

Moss taught himself to play golf in 1937 and earned his living from golf and poker until 1954 when he had to give up golf because of his injuries from a near-fatal auto accident. After he played Nick the Greek at the Horseshoe in 1949, Moss remained in Las Vegas, playing poker there and on the road. When Bradshaw interviewed him in 1973 a few days before the World Series began, Moss was managing the Aladdin Hotel's poker room where Puggy Pearson, Doyle Brunson, Jack Straus and Amarillo Slim were playing high-stakes poker. "I'm sixty-seven and I'm still in there swinging," Moss said of his chances of winning the title again. "Virgie wouldn't want all that money to go nowhere but Texas, and I mean Odessa. When it comes to winnin', I got me a one-track mind." He proved his point in 1974.

In addition to his three championship titles, Moss placed in WSOP events 25 times. "For the last eight years of his life, Johnny played at table 13 at the Horseshoe and finished his legendary career the way it started—living the game of poker," Albrecht noted.

## Highlights

Five preliminary events were played in 1974. Bill Boyd won the five-card stud title; Jimmy Casella won the seven-card razz and seven-card stud events; Amarillo Slim Preston won at no-limit hold'em; and Sailor Roberts won at deuce-to-seven draw. Johnny Moss received a silver cup and a gold bracelet with his name engraved on it.

1974 World Champion Johnny Moss (l) and 1973 World Champion Puggy Pearson playing at one of the two tables in the 16-player field at the 1974 World Series of Poker.

Becky Binion watching Johnny Moss (l) and Puggy Pearson (r) during the 1974 World Series of Poker at Binion's Horseshoe, Las Vegas.

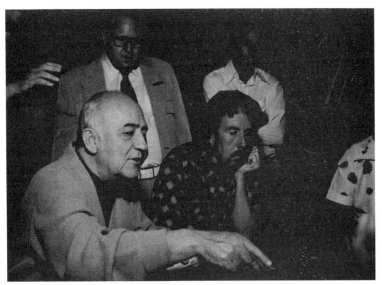

1982 World Champion Jack Straus (r) contemplating the play of 1974 World Champion Johnny Moss during the 1974 WSOP.

Road gambler Bob Hooks (l) and oilman Crandall Addington, runner-up in the championship event, at the 1974 World Series of Poker.

# 1975 World Championship Event
## 6th World Series of Poker
### Number of Entries: 21

———— The Championship Table ————

| The Finalists | Hometown |
|---|---|
| Sailor Roberts | San Angelo, TX |
| Bob Hooks | Edgewood, TX |

Other players included Doyle Brunson, Jimmy Casella, Puggy Pearson and Amarillo Slim Preston.

———————— The Last Hand ————————

| Roberts' Cards | Hooks' Cards |
|---|---|

## How It Happened
Sailor Roberts had about three-fourths of the chips before the last hand began. He and Bob Hooks got all their chips in before the flop. The board cards for the last hand are unknown, but Roberts' pocket nines held up to win the championship for him.

## Highlights
Four preliminary events were played: seven-card razz, won by Sam Angel; deuce-to-seven draw, won by Billy Baxter; no-limit hold'em, won by Jay Heimowitz; and seven-card stud, won by Johnny Moss.

"Sailor was a great player. He was very generous with his money, too. Gave away most of it before he died."

— Amarillo Slim Preston

| The Finish | Prize Money | |
| --- | --- | --- |
| 1st Roberts | $210,000 | |
| 2nd Hooks | -0- | |

## The Road Gamblers

Sailor Roberts traveled the poker circuit in the '60s and '70s with Bobby Hoff, Doyle Brunson, Bob Hooks, Amarillo Slim and the other road gamblers who plied their trade on the dusty back roads of Texas, Louisiana and anywhere else they could find a "good" game. A good game was one with a "live one" in it, maybe a Texas oilman or a wealthy businessman.

"Some of the road gamblers traveled together and played off the same bankroll like Bobby Hoff, Carl McKelvey and Sailor Roberts did," Cowboy Wolford wrote in *Cowboys, Gamblers & Hustlers*. "Everybody was aware of who was playing the same money, but that didn't bother anybody. They played their own hands.

"We traveled to poker games just like cowboys went to rodeos. Some rodeos were bigger than others and some poker games were bigger than others but still, if the right people showed up a small game could become a big game. The 'right people' meant anybody that didn't gamble for a living like all the rest of us.

"Let's say that Mac knew somebody from Waco who had money, what we called a 'producer.' He'd made a call or two and we'd drive to Waco to get in the game with him. We didn't travel to games just to play against each other—there were always a few businessmen from the area who had money and weren't top players. They're the ones we wanted to play with—they were the producers of the road show. Or a big oilman might drop by, have a few drinks, and throw a party. While his wells were producing black gold, he was producing greenbacks at the poker table.

"Road gamblers dressed nice back then, jackets and silk shirts—no tee shirts or baseball caps like today—neat haircuts, manicured nails, gold jewelry. A lot of them were married, owned homes, had children. But they didn't haul their wives around to the gambling joints, I guess because poker was mostly a men's game."

# 1976 World Championship Event
## 7th World Series of Poker
### Number of Entries: 22

——— The Championship Table ———

| **The Finalists** | **Hometown** |
| --- | --- |
| Doyle Brunson | Lubbock, TX |
| Jesse Alto | Houston, TX |

Other players included Jimmy Casella, Johnny Moss, Sailor Roberts, Bob Hooks, Crandall Addington, Amarillo Slim Preston and Howard "Tahoe" Andrew.

——————— The Last Hand ———————

**Brunson's Cards**      **Alto's Cards**

——— Flop ——————— Turn ——— River

## The Finish    Prize Money
1st  Brunson   $220,000
2nd Alto       -0-

## How It Happened
### by Doyle Brunson
I had just beaten Jesse Alto, who was a strong guy, in a big pot and I had three-quarters of the chips. Jesse was steaming—he was a notorious steamer. He raised the pot and I called him with the 10-2 of spades. Jesse had an A-J. He hit aces and jacks on the flop, and I made two tens. There was one spade on the board, as I recall.

Jesse bet and I called him. Then a deuce fell off and I moved in on him. And I caught another 10 on the river.

## Highlights
Prior to winning the championship tournament, Brunson, who moved from Texas to Las Vegas in 1973, won the deuce-to-seven draw preliminary event. Winners of the other six preliminary tournaments were Howard "Tahoe" Andrew, who won both of the no-limit hold'em events; Perry Green, ace-to-five draw; Johnny Moss, seven-card stud; Doc Green, seven-card stud split; and Walter Smiley, seven-card stud.

"You see, I'm a gambler. I'll always be one. I couldn't be anything else. So, my life will always be filled with wins and losses. I wouldn't have it any other way. It's exciting." — Doyle Brunson

"Through it all, I've learned that, in life, a man's not beaten even though he's all in." — Doyle Brunson

# Doyle "Texas Dolly" Brunson
## The Warrior Returns to the Arena
### Interview with a Champ (1998) by Dana Smith

With a staccato of barks and energetic yo-yo jumps, Casper and Cutie greeted us at the front door of Doyle Brunson's elegant home in Las Vegas, where he lives with Louise, his wife of 40 years. During the hour that Linda Johnson and I spent with the legendary gambler, his two petite canine companions never left his side. It was a time to relax and reminisce about the good ol' days with a living legend, to talk about *the* book, the World Series of Poker, golf and sports handicapping.

Brunson created some waves this year (1998) at the World Series of Poker when, after a 20-year hiatus from tournament competition, he made a triumphant return to the arena where he previously had won so many battles, including back-to-back victories in the championship event in '76 and '77. With the indomitable spirit of a world-class competitor, Brunson won the 1998 razz title (his eighth gold bracelet), placed second in the pot-limit Omaha event, and came in third in the deuce to seven draw tournament, bringing the number of his final-table finishes to 19. The tournament reporter described him as one of the "titans of poker"—add the word "legend" and you have a verbal duo that approximates the stature of Brunson in the world of poker, *his* world. This year at the World Series he drew a seat at the same table with Matt Damon, star of the movie *Rounders*. At one point, most of the cameras were focused on Damon, but to Johnson and me and the rest of the poker community, "Texas Dolly" was the real celebrity at that table.

In his quietly understated style, the amiable, soft-spoken Southern gentleman, author and player talked about his poker odyssey from the dimly lit backrooms of Texas to the glitzy casinos of Las Vegas. But poker isn't the only game in which the legendary gambler excels. When Johnson and I interviewed him, Brunson had just won a big-money golf match in which he and Mike Sexton took on Huck Seed and Howard Lederer. We began at the first tee and then moved on to poker talk at the later greens.

*Your golf bet has been the talk of the poker community.*

Has it? I haven't played in several years, but they offered us a game that I thought we just had to play, so I went out and practiced for about a week. It was a scramble. Mike and I would be taking our best shot between the two of us, and Huck and Howard would be taking their best shot. But they were shooting from the blue tees and we were playing from the red tees, the ladies' tees.

*They figured you were over-the-hill?! I heard that it came down to the 16th hole and you made a 35-foot putt that unnerved them and their teeoff from the next hole wasn't too good.*

Yes, after that putt we won the next two holes and came out winner by one stroke. Actually, I didn't think it would be that close, but they really played well.

*Did you have a big wager riding on the deal?*

The total bets amounted to almost half a million. We had a gallery going around with us—there must have been 20 or 30 carts out there with 50 to 100 people, and a lot of them were betting.

*What's the biggest golf bet you've ever made?*

I don't know, I've had a lot of $300,000-$400,000 matches. In this particular one with Sexton, we had $168,000 on a five-way Nassau with two down presses. That's about $800,000 you could've won if you'd won every bet that was possible ... or lost. It's pretty hard to win that decisively, though. I actually thought we'd win them all, but we only won two out of the five bets, $336,000.

*Mike Caro told us that when you were writing Super/System, you purchased almost an entire publishing company, spending incredible amounts of money just to get the book published. Did you ever break even on it?*

Probably by now, maybe (grinning). We had planned to publish more books, but it didn't quite work out that way.

*What inspired you to do it?*

There were publishing companies that wanted me to write it and they'd publish the book, but I'd heard horror stories about guys writing books and never being paid their royalties. I decided that I would do it, but I said, "You have to let me distribute the books. I can get them printed as cheaply as you can, so I'll have them printed and give them to you and then I'll know how many books you've sold." But they wouldn't even consider that, so I thought well, hell, I'll just do it all myself. Then I set up a publishing company and bought all these machines and things. We rented a building and hired a staff, about 12 employees, and brought a guy in to market it and we ran ads in every major newspaper in America, I guess. Then we found out that at $100 a book, the market was pretty limited. I guess that was kind of the beginning of the end. We weren't making enough money to keep the thing going, so we decided to close it down. That's how it's become what it is today ... you know, just a few outlets that sell it. I think we're in the eighth or ninth edition now, and each printing was anywhere from 5,000 to 10,000 copies.

*One positive offshoot of the book is that it said to the public, "It's okay to educate people about how to play poker."*

Yes, it created a lot of players. It made good players out of poor players, and *real* good players out of good ones.

*Do you think that a weak player can get as much out of the book as one who is an intermediate or advanced player?*

Yes, especially back in those days. There's so much more knowledge out there now, you know, and players know so many things that nobody knew back then because of all the books and programs nowadays. I think the greatest thing that ever happened to poker was Mike putting that poker program on the computer (Caro's Poker Probe). If I'd had that back when I was young ... I mean, I just can't imagine that players don't use it all the time.

*So, your poker lessons were a little bit more expensive than they might have been today?*

Yes, although I was a little bit ahead of my time as a player. That's probably the reason why I was the dominant no-limit player during that period of time. But today, a lot of players have the knowledge that I had back then.

*What was it like to be a road warrior?*

It was tough, that's what it was. You had to be a very dedicated person—you had to have a single-minded purpose just to play poker. We'd drive 500 miles to play in a $5-$10 blind game. There weren't that many games so you had to go to just about all of them just to make a living. It was all no-limit poker back in Texas, Oklahoma, and the South.

Sailor (Roberts) and Slim (Preston) and I were partners, so we traveled together. There was a sort of nucleus of professional players, about 15 guys, who played the circuit from one town to the other. Johnny Moss was one of the primary ones, Bob Hooks played a lot, and Bill Smith was there, too. And Jack Straus—he was a great guy and one of the most entertaining people I've ever known in my life. There was a camaraderie back then that was almost like a fraternity. We had good times.

*What do you mean by "partners?"*

We played off the same bankroll. Nowadays you hear all this commotion about partners. We were partners, but we didn't *play* partners. I mean, we never did anything wrong. Being bankroll partners was to our disadvantage because everybody knew about it. We would never make any out-of-line plays like one guy betting and the other one raising or they wouldn't let us play with them.

*Was it dangerous?*

Oh, yeah. You had to win the money, you had to collect the money, and then you had to get out of town with the money. You had to worry about getting arrested, getting robbed, getting cheated ... it was a different world back then. I've been robbed probably four times. Twice people just came into the game and held us up and once, a guy sneaked up behind me. Then one time a bunch of guys jumped on me as I was coming out the door. That was the only time I really got hurt and they wouldn't even let me give them my money! They just seemed intent on knocking me out. They kicked me in the head and hit me with pipes. For some reason, I've never been knocked out; I've taken some awful blows, but I just don't go out. I had the money in my pocket and would've just handed it to them gladly, but they kept on beating on me. I started grabbing dirt and throwing it up into their faces. I finally got up and whacked a couple of them and the rest of them ran off.

*You mentioned that in the old days, there were two busts during the home games. Were there any shootings?*

One time a long time ago, a guy got killed. It wasn't exactly a robbery, though. A man just came busting in and shot the guy. One of the funny stories happened when we were playing in Austin, Texas. Suddenly, windows broke all over the house and seven guys with shot guns came at us from every angle. They lined us all up against the wall and made us drop our pants. Some girl there said she'd never seen so many naked butts and shaking knees in her life! So there we all were, half naked, and the robbers would always pick on the biggest guy, which usually was me. This little bitty guy—he was about five feet tall and his eyes were glazed over—punched me in the stomach with his shot gun and asked, "Who runs this game?" I said, "I don't know." (It was an unwritten law that you didn't snitch on anybody.) Then wham! He hit me on the side of the head with the butt of his gun and repeated, "Who runs this game?" Again I said, "I don't know." He had one of those old guns and he pulled the hammer back and cocked it and put it right up to my temple. "Who runs this game?" he asked. "That guy right over there!" I answered.

*That got your attention! Do you miss those days?*

Well, you know, they were fun. And I was young and full of energy and ambition and I just wanted to play. I can't say as I miss them, but they were very exciting. I wouldn't want to do it now, but back then it was a great life.

*Who do you really respect in the world of poker today?*

Anybody who puts their feet under the table! I don't mind playing with just about anybody. I really consider myself lucky to have the ability to play because for most people it seems like about 50 years of age is the cutoff point. That's when their game starts going down. The other day, somebody said to me, "You've lost 10 percent of your game." I said, "Well, yeah, but fortunately I was 30 percent ahead of everybody else to start with." Of course, I think that Chip (Reese) was probably the best of the modern poker players, but he doesn't play much now, so I don't think I could consider him to be the best player anymore. You have to have a desire to play, and he just doesn't have that much desire any more.

*Do you still love playing poker?*

Not like I did. I used to like it at Binion's, but there aren't that many games there anymore. Somebody told me that you have to play to where it hurts if you lose, and I think there's a certain element of truth in that. The stakes have to be high enough that it really hurts you if you lose—the amount could be $100 for some people and $100,000 for others—that's what makes the game interesting. Maybe you get to the point, too, where you don't really need the money anymore and so it has to be a really high game to get you stimulated.

*I've heard stories about the big games you used to play with Bob Stupak, Lyle Berman and others. Does any of that go on now?*

Yes, it does, usually when Lyle's around. It seems like he's the catalyst. When he's in town, the group gathers around. Bobby (Baldwin) usually will play and when he plays, then Chip will play, and then Howard (Lederer) and David (Grey) and Johnny (Chan) and some others will join in. We play $50,000 change-in, probably. The group decides what games they want to play, usually two different games. And a lot of times these days, it's limit poker.

*You don't usually play the smaller events at the Series, but this year you did. What made you decide to play them?*

One reason was that some guys had passed me by and I wanted to keep my name towards the top of the list. Another reason was that they were putting out these lists (odds sheets) with the favorites on them—and they didn't even have me in the top eight! I have nothing against women poker players, but they had a few women in front of me. "I'm gonna have to do something about that," I said. So, instead of playing in the side games, I played in the tournaments for the first time in 20 years.

*When you and T. J. Cloutier were heads up in the $2,500 pot-limit Omaha event, which he won with an ace kicker, something was mentioned about striking a deal on the end, but you declined. Why?*

There were two reasons. To start with, it isn't that the money doesn't mean anything to me, but it doesn't put any pressure on me, whereas it might put some pressure on somebody else who's trying to win it—it might change their play a little bit. The other thing is that he had a slight lead on me two-handed. The person who's behind can't make a deal, that would be silly. One pot and things could be reversed. I'll make a deal according to the chips, but if I'm behind I won't. If I'm ahead, I love to make a deal.

The last tournament I won at Binion's was a hold'em tournament and there were two of us left. The other guy couldn't play at all; he was really a bad player. I had about a 2-to-1 lead over him in chips and we made a deal. Then somebody asked, "Well,

Doyle, why did you make a deal?" While he couldn't play, he was raising $80,000 more on every hand. One time when I made a stand, he threw his hand away with a 7-2—and he'd raised me $80,000 with it! Well, I mean that guy is capable of beating you! Suppose he wins two or three hands, or I'm not holding any cards and just keep letting him run over me—I don't have a big enough ego that I think I can't be beaten. So I made a deal with him based on our chips.

*Who are some of today's finest tournament players?*

T. J.'s a fine player, probably the best tournament player today. And of course, you've gotta go with Berry (Johnston). But there's just such a difference between tournament players and money game players, you know. You look at some of the finest tournament players and when they get into money games, they have trouble winning. People just lick their chops when they see a couple of them sit down in their ring game. I don't understand why a player can't win at tournaments and in ring games, too.

The question I've been asked the most over the years is, "What does it take to make a good poker player?" Who knows what it takes? I don't know. It's an innate ability that you can't explain. It's something inside you that causes you to pull away from the field. I do know that with just the knowledge and ability to play, you can play at a certain level, but you have to have that "something" inside you to pull away. It's a sixth sense, or an inclination to win, or something. How can you say, for instance, that I am a better player than David Sklansky or Mike Caro? I think that obviously I probably am, but the two of them are the foremost authorities on poker. They know everything, the situations and what you're supposed to do, yet when it comes time to perform them, they can't do it. They chill up or something happens.

*You tried to explain what makes a great poker player in Super/System.*

That explanation is the best one I've ever thought of. It's a sense of *recall* that great players have. You recall what happened the last time you were in this same situation with a player of that caliber. Starting off, you put players in categories by watching their table mannerisms, the way they handle their chips, the way they handle their cards, and so on. You say to yourself that this guy's a certain kind of player, and that guy's a certain kind of player, and then when you get in a pot with them, you recall—subconsciously—the last time you were playing with a guy like that and a similar situation came up. So, you play according to the way the guy played previously. And that's the best way I can explain it.

*Dewey (Tomko) told me that you and he used to hold Bible classes for players during poker games. Do you still do that?*

No, not like we used to do. We had some religious celebrities, Rosie Greer and Roger McDuff, come out and it was a pretty big thing for a number of years. I think it did a lot of good and helped people. A lot of poker players don't go to church, you know, and it gave them an opportunity to talk to pastors on a one-to-one basis, ask questions and get answers. Bob Tremain, a friend of mine from Texas that I went to school with, has been coming out here during the *World Series* for about the past 15 years. He goes around and just talks to people. A lot of players have problems and nobody to tell them to, you know. I think Danny Robison is holding some classes at his home these days, too.

*What is your advice for new poker players?*

It's different than it used to be, but I can't imagine a better life. My son Todd is a good example. I didn't want him to be a poker player, but he has become one. You're your own boss, make your own hours, and should make plenty of money. And in Nevada at least, it's respectable. Back where I come from, they still turn up their nose at you. My college won't put me in its Hall of Fame because I'm a professional gambler. That aggravated me at first, but it's not that big a deal to me. A lot of my friends petitioned them to put me in it, but there's somebody there that's really an objector.

*Actually, I think it's somebody you beat in a game back in Texas! Has there been a highlight in your poker career?*

The highlight was always the World Series of Poker. To win that is the best compliment that you can have.

*Is the WSOP tougher to beat these days?*

Oh, sure. The players are so good. I mean, those kids have learned all the tournament moves, they know how to play.

*Is this a time in your life when you can just kick back?*

Oh, no! I'm fixin' to go to work right now. I'm into sports handicapping. I work on the computer on the baseball statistics and study them a lot. And football season's coming up . . .

# 1977 World Championship Event
## 8th World Series of Poker
### Number of Entries: 34

―――――― The Championship Table ――――――

| The Finalists | Hometown |
|---|---|
| "Bones" Berland | Las Vegas, NV |
| Doyle Brunson | Lubbock, TX |
| Milo Jacobson | Texas |
| Andy Moore | Sarasota, FL |
| Sailor Roberts | San Angelo, TX |

―――――――― The Last Hand ――――――――

**Brunson's Cards**          **Berland's Cards**

―――――― Flop ―――――― Turn ―――― River

| The Finish | Prize Money |
| --- | --- |
| 1st Brunson | $340,000 |
| 2nd Berland | -0- |
| 3rd Jacobson | -0- |
| 4th Moore | -0- |

## How It Happened
### by Doyle Brunson

I was in the big blind and had 10-2 against Bones Berland. The flop came out 10-8-5. I checked and he checked. He had eights and fives. The fourth card was a deuce. I bet, he moved in on me, and I called. The last card was another 10. So, in both hands (in 1976 and 1977), I made a full house with 10-2.

## Highlights

1977 is the first year for which there are complete figures for the World Series. $806,800 in prize money was awarded to 366 entries. Twelve preliminary tournaments were played prior to the championship event. Doyle Brunson won one of the two seven-card stud split events and Johnny Moss won one of the two seven-card stud events. Bobby Baldwin made his first WSOP splash by winning two events, deuce-to-seven draw and seven-card stud.

The first ladies-only World Series tournament was played in 1977. The victor was Jackie McDaniels, who was awarded $5,580 for winning the inaugural Women's Championship of Poker. The game was seven-card stud.

"How did you guys fit in with Doyle, Amarillo Slim, and some of these old characters?" — Entertainment Tonight to Matt Damon and Edward Norton at the 1998 World Series of Poker, which the screen stars played to promote their new movie, *Rounders.*

"I don't know that we did fit in." — Matt Damon

"We're skinnier than most of them." — Edward Norton

1975 champion Sailor Roberts (l) and Bob Hooks (r) at the 1976
WSOP with Benny Binion and Steve Wynn looking on.

Amarillo Slim Preston, dealer Kenny Lambert, and Sailor Roberts
(l-r, front) at the 1976 WSOP with tournament director Eric Drache,
"Satellite Sam" Gamburg and Doyle Brunson (l-r, back).

Crandall Addington (r) shaking hands with Sailor Roberts (l) as Doyle Brunson looks on during the 1976 World Series of Poker.

Runner-up Jesse Alto (l) playing heads up against 1976 champion Doyle Brunson at the championship table at the 1976 World Series of Poker. Brunson won his second title in 1977. Alto went on to finish third to Jack Keller and Byron "Cowboy" Wolford in 1984.

# 1978 World Championship Event
## 9th World Series of Poker
### Number of Entries: 42

———— The Championship Table ————

| The Finalists | Hometown |
|---|---|
| Jesse Alto | Houston, TX |
| Crandall Addington | San Antonio, TX |
| Bobby Baldwin | Tulsa, OK |
| Buck Buchanan | Killeen, TX |
| Louis Hunsucker | Houston, TX |

———— The Last Hand ————

**Baldwin's Cards**     **Addington's Cards**

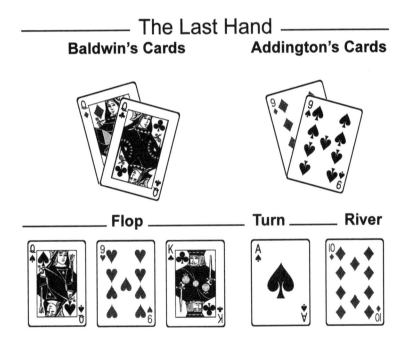

———— Flop ———— Turn ———— River

| The Finish | Prize Money |
|---|---|
| 1st Baldwin | $210,000 |
| 2nd Addington | $ 84,800 |
| 3rd Hunsucker | $ 63,000 |
| 4th Buchanan | $ 42,000 |
| 5th Alto | $ 21,000 |

## How It Happened
### by Tom McEvoy

In the final hand of the 1978 Series, 27-year-old Bobby Baldwin faced off against Crandall Addington. Baldwin was considered to be the best no-limit hold'em player in the world at that time, and Addington was a respected high-limit Texas gambler. Going into the final hand, Baldwin had a substantial chip lead—$370,000 to $50,000 for Addington. If Addington had won the final hand, he would have had at least a fighting chance with $100,000 in chips against Baldwin's $320,000. When Addington flat-called with 9-9, Baldwin raised $10,000 with Q-Q and Addington moved in the rest of his chips. The flop came with both a queen and a nine, set over set in the final hand! Addington was reduced to having to catch a magic nine which, of course, he missed.

The betting was rather unusual in that two nines wasn't the type of hand to slow-play and yet that's what Addington did before the flop. He must have thought that Baldwin would make an aggressive play and then he could come over the top, which indeed is what happened. Addinton's decision to reraise when Baldwin raised $10,000 certainly was justified. One way or the other, all the chips were destined to go into the pot on the flop when they both flopped sets—there was no way for Addington to avoid his dismal destiny.

Baldwin, who went on to become the President and CEO of Mirage Resorts, was inducted into the Poker Hall of Fame in 2003.

## Highlights
1978 was the first year that the prize pool was divided among the top five players. Barbara Freer, who won the women's title, became the first woman in WSOP history to enter the championship event.

# 1979 World Championship Event
## 10th World Series of Poker
### Number of Entries: 54

## ———— The Championship Table ————

| The Finalists | Hometown |
|---|---|
| Crandall Addington | San Antonio, TX |
| Bobby Baldwin | Tulsa, OK |
| Hal Fowler | Los Angeles, CA |
| George Huber | Las Vegas, NV |
| Sam Moon | Corpus Christi, NM |
| Johnny Moss | Las Vegas, NV |
| Sam Petrillo | Van Nuys, CA |
| Bobby Hoff | Houston, TX |

## ———— The Last Hand ————

**Fowler's Cards**    **Hoff's Cards**

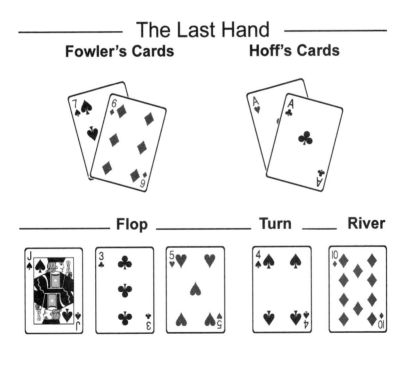

———— Flop ———— Turn ——— River

| The Finish | Prize Money |
|---|---|
| 1st  Fowler | $270,000 |
| 2nd  Hoff | $108,000 |
| 3rd  Huber | $ 81,000 |
| 4th  Moon | $ 54,000 |
| 5th  Moss | $ 27,000 |
| 6th  Petrillo | -0- |
| 7th  Addington | -0- |
| 8th  Baldwin | -0- |

## How It Happened

"In the final pot," Bobby Hoff recalls, "I raised with two aces and Hal called with a 7-6 offsuit. I bet half of my money on the flop and he called the bet. Hal caught a four on the turn to make the gutshot straight and win the title." The irony is that probably no other player at the final table would have called a preflop raise with only a seven-high hand, especially against the legendary Hoff.

## Highlights

Bobby Baldwin, the defending champion, went out in eighth place. Holding pocket eights, Baldwin bet when the flop came with an eight to give him trips. Sam Moon, who had pocket aces, raised Baldwin all-in on the flop. When an ace came on the turn, it sealed Baldwin's fate in an unusual case of set over set at the final table. The first player to be knocked out of the 1979 Series was Jack Straus, who went on to win the championship in 1982. The first WSOP final table to be video-taped since the 1973 video premier, the tape featured comments from Kenny Rogers, whose song "The Gambler" was a big hit at that time.

For the first time in World Series of Poker history, an amateur won the championship. Oldtimers give Fowler little credit for being a world-class player, dismissing his victory as a matter of his getting lucky at the right time against the venerable Hoff. The 1983 WSOP brochure saw Fowler's victory in a different light: "The WSOP has produced some notable surprises in the thirteen years since it was established in 1970. Perhaps one of the most unexpected turns of events was the capture in 1979 of the World Championship title by softspoken amateur Hal Fowler, who started the tournament as a

40-to-1 underdog. However he survived 33 hours of grueling play to wrest the laurels from Bobby 'The Wizard' Hoff in a memorable head-to-head contest.

"The general consensus of the tournament staff and fellow poker players was that Fowler's dark horse win would increase interest in the Series and result in an influx of new blood. They couldn't have called it better. In 1980 Buffalo Butch and Maverick Mike Bamrich strolled in right off a Nebraska cattle ranch and plunked down their $10,000 each. And Colette Doherty, that year's Irish Champion, who was known only as Madam X until her offcial entry, flew in from Dublin with a large press entourage."

The Poker Hall of Fame was founded in 1979 with the induction of seven charter members—Johnny Moss, three-time World Champion of Poker; Nick "The Greek" Dandolos, a classic high-stakes gambler; Felton "Corky" McCorquodale, the Texas gambler who introduced hold'em to Las Vegas in 1963; Red Winn, quintessential poker player; Sid Wyman, former co-owner of the Sands, Riviera and Dunes hotels; Wild Bill Hickok, famous for getting killed holding aces and eights; and Edmond Hoyle, whose name has become synonymous with the rules of card games.

Eleven preliminary tournaments were played, including the premier of mixed doubles, a seven-card stud event that remained on the schedule through 1983. The winners were Doyle Brunson, 1976-77 World Champion, and Starla Brodie, who went on to win the ladies championship in 1995.

Little is known about Fowler's life since 1979, except that the 52-year-old amateur poker player apparently returned to his position as a public relations representative in Los Angeles. Bobby Hoff's story is a colorful saga of victory and defeat in the green felt jungle of high-stakes poker.

"Let's face it, gambling is a very romantic activity. We all daydream about people doing something we are a little bit afraid to do, and we make heroes out of those who pull it off." — Jack Binion

"The world's got plenty of lawyers. What we need is a few more gamblers." — George Huber

# Bobby Hoff
## A Sunny Day after a Long Night
### Interview with a Champ (1997)
### by Dana Smith

I didn't recognize him when he walked into a local health food emporium for our luncheon interview, this man who has been called the world's greatest no-limit hold'em player. Dressed in Ivy League sportcoat, starched shirt and freshly creased denims, he appeared more the businessman than the poker player in billed cap whom I had seen at the World Series of Poker the day before hovering over a pile of chips at the $25-$50 pot-limit game. But he is at home in both milieus: Almost everyday, he makes the trek across town to dine on organically grown veggies, each time bringing back a take-out box for his evening meal at the close of his poker session in the big side-game section of the WSOP.

With emotion that is off-limits at the poker table, he joined me at the dining table, where he spoke with a quiver in his voice about losing his dear friend, Sailor Roberts; about the recent loss of his mother; and about losing the World Series of Poker championship in 1979. But to soften the suffering of loss has come a renewed confidence in winning the game of a lifetime. Bobby Hoff is a survivor, a man who has recovered his life from the rubble of drugs, alcohol, personal loss, and debt—with the help of his friends.

In sharp contrast to the life that he leads today as a working pro is his checkered past as a road gambler. "The night before a game, I would put two lines of cocaine on the bed stand," he confided. "Then I'd put an ashtray over them so the humidity wouldn't get to them too bad. When I woke up, I'd roll over, take the two rails of cocaine, order some cognac from the bell desk, and lay there till the swelling in my wrist went down, maybe force an egg down, and then I'd go play poker."

These days Hoff plays the $40-$80 and $60-$120 games at the Commerce Club, where he works as a silent prop. "I usually come in around 3:00 in the afternoon and play until about 10:00 at night, so I keep pretty regular hours. It's a great job, there's never any hassle. If it were any other kind of job, I couldn't handle it." Twice a day, Hoff takes about 60 vitamin supplements with his favorite juice, a liquid tonic that he concocts at his home in Downey, California, on his juice extractor from carrot, apple, parsley, celery and ginger. The rest of his diet includes fresh vegetables and an occasional serving of fish or chicken.

Even now he speaks with emotion about losing the 1979 World Series title to amateur Hal Fowler. I listened empathetically as he recounted the story of one of the most famous final tables ever played at the WSOP. Fowler is only one of three amateurs ever to win the WSOP championship; Hoff is considered to be one of the world's greatest no-limit hold'em players.

So how did the amateur prevail over the pros? According to T.J. Cloutier, "You could have played as good as God and still not have beaten Hal on that day." And it wasn't only Hoff that Fowler erased from the tote board: At the final table was one of the most awesome lineups in the annals of the WSOP—Bobby Baldwin, Crandall Addington and Johnny Moss, among others. But before Hoff relates that story, let's pick up his personal life years before his run at the title, when many of the legendary players whose names are engraved in the stone tablets of poker history were making their mark. His is a big-stack, little-stack, no-stack story of the ups and downs of fame and fortune on a green felt elevator.

*Not many poker players have such a healthy regimen. How did you develop the discipline to turn your life around?*

I never paid any attention to my health until I discovered that I have chronic hepatitis. The best friend I've ever had, Sailor Roberts, died from sclerosis caused by hepatitis. We used to do drugs together. I'm lucky that I discovered three years ago that I have the disease. It has probably saved my life because I've changed the way that I live. All the people (except one) that I used to do drugs with have hepatitis. One doctor told me that I probably would get sclerosis in about two to 10 years, at which time I could either have a liver transplant or die. I didn't like those odds, so I looked into alternative medicine and found a doctor who put me on massive doses of vitamin C, Shetaki mushroom extract and Silimarin. Then I changed my diet and started exercising.

*Before you began regaining your health, you were a road gambler. What kind of a life was that?*

Starting in 1961, I was never gone from Las Vegas for more than six months, but I was never there longer than about 18 months. I lived continually tooting and drinking for 20, 30, 40 hours at a time—I'd sleep for a few hours and then do it all over again. Around 1979 or '80, I started shooting cocaine and I did that for about seven or eight years. I was very lucky to live through it; I could have died with every shot. Most likely, that was when I picked up the hepatitis, and I was pretty lucky not to have picked up AIDS, too. It wasn't all luck, however, because I was kinda rich for a junkie and I always used clean syringes. In Nevada, you have to sign your name in a register book when you buy syringes. I went into White Cross drugs one morning at about 4:00 and the last three signatures in the book were mine. When I was doing that stuff, I would go on binges for a week or three weeks and then I would stop for a month or two, and then I was on binges again. I lost 90 pounds on one of them. People thought that I had cancer, I looked so bad. When people think that you're going to die, they avoid you because it makes them feel uneasy. They also were afraid that I was going to borrow money from them.

*You were doing some borrowing in those days?*

Yes. When I finally quit drugs in 1987, I owed $150,000. Probably $20,000 or $30,000 of that money I didn't even remember borrowing. A lot of it was in $100 and $200 loans. Just before I got on the plane to go to Los Angeles that year (when they started playing hold'em there), I had to ask a friend for $10 to pay my bar tab—and I owed $150,000! It took me five years before I finally came across the last guy who said, "Bobby, I guess you've forgotten that $200 you got from me."

*How did you get off the stuff?*

My friends Steve Lott and Carl McKelvey gave me one more chance. They played something like a tough-love program with me. I guess I realized that I had gone all the way to the bottom, that I couldn't sink any farther. Fortunately, I have this ability to play. You see, people such as airline pilots or anybody else who has a real talent, especially one that will make money, have a good chance of getting off drugs. It's easier for them because they have something to live for, something to occupy themselves. You can get so much into playing games, or whatever it is that you love, that it can take the place of drugs. Plus, there's a pride thing. It was pride that made me quit. You can't go back to it, either, because it's terrifying. After you've done cocaine for a number of years, it builds up in your body. You get the first rush and then you get this terrible paranoia and it happens every single time.

*Are you happier now than you have been?*

I feel pretty good. I lost my mother and my friend Sailor, but I feel good about myself. I've beat the coke addiction for 10 years; I quit smoking seven years ago; and I've changed my diet and lost weight. It gives you confidence that you can accomplish other things.

*I've heard that you're the best no-limit hold'em player in the world. True?*

How can you tell who's the best? Bobby Baldwin is the best no-limit hold'em player that I've ever played with. Doyle Brunson and Stuey Ungar are great, too. And Sailor was a wonderful player, totally unique. I learned a lot about poker from Sailor and Doyle.

*Did you also learn things in college?*

I had a golf scholarship to the University of Texas in 1958 and I started playing poker when I got there—won $8,000 the first semester and thought I was rich. I didn't go back to the golf course for 10 years. I also thought for sure that I was the best poker player in the world, but when I stopped playing with those university boys, I discovered that I wasn't.

*How did you find that out?*

I come from a little town in Texas that used to be a wide open gambling town. Victoria had a population of about 50,000 and there were three full-fledged casinos. The town had the most millionaires per capita in the U. S. in 1957. There were poker games everywhere, 24 hours a day. After I had lost all my money that I had won at the university, I went to work dealing blackjack and craps and it paid me pretty good, about $40 a night. They paid you every night in cash, whether you needed it or not. When I left the club at night, I'd take my money and play poker until I got broke or had to go back to work. Then in 1964, I picked up a copy of Thorpe's *Beat The Dealer*. So, a friend and I learned the ten-count, quit our jobs, and went to Las Vegas with a $200 bankroll. We started out playing for quarters, dollars, whatever, and we finally built it up to $10,000.

Then I got drunk and lost it all in one night.

We both started working as shills and worked our way up to dealing blackjack at the Downtown casinos. We would take our tokes, usually between $2 and $10, and play blackjack with them. I had a system, especially with a real small bankroll. I would bet 50 cents, call for the cocktail waitress, order a pack of cigarettes and a drink, and then I would bet one-half of my bankroll when the deck was favorable, which might be $2 or $10 or if I was winning, several hundred dollars. Eventually, we would make a little strike. We built our bankroll back up to about $10,000 and wound up in Reno. It was Christmas Eve, and we were going home to Victoria for the holidays. I got drunk just before we left and lost it all again in one night. My friend had hidden away $200 so we had enough to get home. Then I met a man from Corpus Christi who had some money and we started playing seriously. We formed a team and played blackjack from about 1966 until 1970, when we started getting a tremendous amount of heat and were barred from everyplace.

*Is that when you began playing poker again?*

Yes. They opened up a cardroom at the Horseshoe and I started playing pot-limit hold'em, my favorite game. I had managed to squirrel away some money and I lost it all in that game. Goody (James Roy), a legendary player, probably beat me out of about $250,000—he's a wonderful player. But I learned a lot. I had known Sailor for a long time, and he staked me in a bigger game at the Golden Nugget with Bill Boyd and all those guys. We played $5-$10-$25 with a $500 change in. That doesn't sound like a big game now, but it was big enough for Doyle to play in. So, I finally learned how to play—but I never did learn how to take care of the money. Sailor was staking me, so he would take one-half of my play and sometimes he would let me have a quarter of his play. I remember that in one stretch of about 60 days, we won $80,000, and then one day we lost $12,000 and we were broke! And I've spent most of the rest of my life just like that: Win, win, win, win, win—then I'd lose a couple of times and I'd have to get stake money or borrow some.

*Didn't that bother you, the roller coaster ride?*

It didn't bother me much back then because the poker was just every place. Finding a game was no problem—all of the cities in Texas had no-limit and pot-limit hold'em games. Now they play in London, there's one little game in New York, a little game in Paris, they play in Oceanside, there's a couple of little games in Texas, and that's it. How was I supposed to know that it would end? There was so much money around, I didn't worry about being broke, it wasn't a big deal. But it's not that way anymore.

*How has it changed?*

Now it's all limit poker, and that's so much different. It's a very frustrating game because you can't use your talents. Say that the cards are out and your opponent bets. You'd love to lay 2-to-1 that he has you beat, but the pot's laying you 10-to-1, so you have to call. Conversely, when you bluff, your opponent says to himself, "Well, he's probably got me beat, but there's so much money in the pot, if there's any possibility that he's bluffing, I've got to call." And so, the guy that just always calls or always bets is almost as good as somebody that knows something. All the plays in limit poker are like soft double-downs in blackjack, they're so close. It's very frustrating to see lesser players do better than you do—you've played for years and you know clearly that you're better than they are, and that just galls me.

*Speaking of playing against opponents that you out-class, tell me about coming second to Hal Fowler at the 1979 WSOP.*

I got about as tough a beat as you'll ever hear about in a key hand that came up before the final hand. With one card to come, I had two queens and a six kicker; Hal had two jacks with a king kicker. He had all of his money in the pot, and I still had $150,000 in chips. He caught a king on the river to make two pair, kings and jacks. Nobody even remembers that hand. In another one when he was all in, we both had the same straight and I had a flush draw; I didn't make the flush and so we split that pot. Then in another hand, I bluffed at the pot and back-doored a king-high flush; he back-doored an ace-high flush. In the final pot, I raised with two aces and Hal called me with 7-6 offsuit. The flop came J-3-5. I bet half of my money on the flop and he called the bet. Hal caught a four on the turn to make the gutshot straight and win the title.

*Sounds like Lady Luck was on his side that day.*

Yes. You should have seen the final table—Bobby Baldwin, Crandall Addington, George Huber, Sam Petrillo, Sam Moon,

Johnny Moss. Every player at the table was a world-class player except for Hal—and he only had a few chips to start, I think about $2,000 out of $550,000 chips in play. Bobby's as good a player as anybody ever was, and obviously Johnny was a great player. And Hal won that thing! Eric Drache estimated that Hal took 20 Valiums just while we were playing head-up. We must have played head-up for 10 or 12 hours. I won all of the little pots, but every time we had a big confrontation and a big pot, Hal won every single one. After each one of those pots that I told you about, except for the last one, I came back and was in the tournament again.

Having Hal beat me in the *WSOP* had a big effect on my life. I had nightmares for three weeks afterward. I never realized how much I wanted to win until I got down there with a chance to win it. In my life, I've been in many tough spots—I've bluffed my money many times, and I've had a huge amount of rushes. But never have the palms of my hands sweated, except for that one time at the final table. I thought I was playing for the money, but then I realized that I wanted to win it. I still get emotional when I talk about it.

*Luck seems to play quite a role in tournaments.*

Yes, there's a tremendous amount of luck involved in poker tournaments. It's not a good way to gamble. Tournaments are very frustrating. You also lose your time when you play, and you become extremely tired. The only exception is the Big One.

*What advice do you have for rising poker stars?*

There is something that I want to say to the young professional players and the would-be pros that I hope they will seriously consider: The casino and the winning players are *partners*. It costs millions of dollars to get people to come in and support the games. Players who throw their cards at the dealer and act rudely are bad for business. Ambience is what we're selling at the poker table. A lot of people just come to play. If they would honestly admit it to themselves, they would say, "Well, I can't really win, but I love to play poker. I like the company and it's fun and I'm with the boys." But rude players ruin it for them, they ruin it for everybody. And as their "business partner," I object! We are partners—don't mistreat *our* customers. When you mistreat players in a game, they freeze up. They're afraid to play, to make a mistake because somebody's going to get mad. On the other hand, when everybody's laughing and having a good time, the game stays good. Business is good.

# 11th WSOP • 1980
# World Championship Event
## Number of Entries: 73

———— The Championship Table ————

| The Finalists | Hometown |
|---|---|
| Doyle Brunson | Lubbock, TX |
| Charles Dunwoody | Unknown |
| Jay Heimowitz | Bethel, NY |
| Johnny Moss | Las Vegas, NV |
| Stu Ungar | Las Vegas, NV |

———————— The Last Hand ————————

**Ungar's Cards**          **Brunson's Cards**

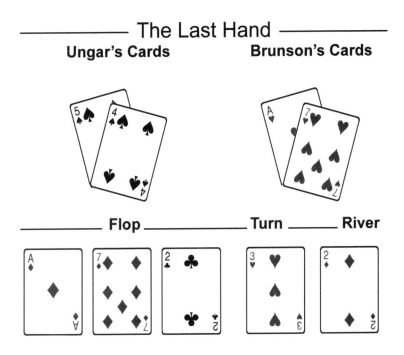

_____ Flop _____ Turn _____ River

| The Finish | Prize Money |
|---|---|
| 1st Ungar | $385,000 |
| 2nd Brunson | $146,000 |
| 3rd Heimowitz | $109,500 |
| 4th Moss | $ 73,000 |
| 5th Dunwoody | $ 36,500 |

## How It Happened
### by Doyle Brunson

The chips were fairly close when the last hand began. I made two mistakes in the same hand, one of the worst plays I've ever made. Before the flop I brought it in for a raise and Stu called, making about $17,000 in the pot. I flopped top two pair. A lot of times in this situation, I would bet big (overbet the pot) to throw off my opponent, but this time I decided to trap Stu and so I only bet the size of the pot, $17,000. Stu called. That was my first mistake.

When a three came on the turn, Stu led at the pot for around $30,000 and I moved all-in. Stu called. That was my second mistake. I should've just flat-called because at the river, when a deuce fell that paired the board and also made a flush possible, Stu would've shut down—and I wouldn't have got broke to the hand.

## Highlights

In 1980 there was $1,788,400 awarded to 846 total entries. Eleven preliminary events were played including seven-card stud, won by Mickey Appleman; draw-high won by Pat Callihan; deuce-to-seven draw won by Sarge Ferris; no-limit hold'em won by Gene Fisher; and seven-card razz won by Lakewood Louie. Road gambler T. "Blondie" Forbes was inducted into the Poker Hall of Fame.

"I'm gonna look bad (on TV) playing hands like that."
— Stu Ungar to Gabe Kaplan at the 1997 WSOP
after losing a large bet with a 9-8.

# 1981 World Championship Event
## 12th World Series of Poker
### Number of Entries: 75

———— The Championship Table ————

| The Finalists | Chip Count | Hometown |
|---|---|---|
| Bobby Baldwin | $128,200 | Las Vegas, NV |
| Gene Fisher | $ 84,700 | El Paso, TX |
| Perry Green | $ 87,900 | Anchorage, AK |
| Jay Heimowitz | $103,000 | Bethel, NY |
| Andy Moore | $ 28,100 | Sarasota, FL |
| Sam Petrillo | $ 67,400 | Van Nuys, CA |
| Bill Smith | $ 82,600 | Roswell, NM |
| Ken "Top Hat" Smith | $114,800 | Dallas, TX |
| Stu Ungar | $ 53,200 | Las Vegas, NV |

———— The Last Hand ————

**Ungar's Cards**     **Green's Cards**

**Flop**     **Turn**     **River**

| The Finish | Prize Money |
|---|---|
| 1st Ungar | $375,000 |
| 2nd Green | $150,000 |
| 3rd Fisher | $ 75,000 |
| 4th Smith, Ken | $ 37,500 |
| 5th Smith, Bill | $ 37,500 |
| 6th Heimowitz | $ 30,000 |
| 7th Baldwin | $ 15,000 |
| 8th Moore | $ 15,000 |
| 9th Petrillo | $ 15,000 |

## How It Happened

Stu Ungar raised before the flop with A-Q. Holding 10-9, Green called the raise. When he flopped a straight draw, Green moved all in on a semibluff. Ungar quickly called with the nut flush draw and two overcards. A queen on the river gave Ungar his second world championship win in a row. Doyle Brunson recalled a key hand played prior to the last hand that could have won the championship for Perry Green: "A ten-deuce almost won a third tournament when Stu Ungar and Perry Green were playing heads up. Perry had more chips than Stuey and they got it all in. The flop came J-9-8 with two clubs. Perry had the 10♣ 2♣, but Stuey had the A♣ J♣. The fourth card was a six and the last one was a blank—but if that six had been a seven, Perry would have won the tournament with a straight and it would have been the third time that a 10-2 had won it. As it turned out, Stuey won a $560,000 pot that turned the tide."

## Highlights

1981 marked the first time the championship event lasted four days rather than three. The added day allowed players extra rest and more action at each level. 1981 also was the first year that all nine finalists at the championship table were awarded prize money. Series total prize money exceeded $2 million, the amount won by a single winner in the title event in 2002.

Bill Boyd, legendary master of five-card stud, was inducted into the Poker Hall of Fame. Boyd was ceremonially dealt the first poker hands at both the Golden Nugget and Mirage cardrooms.

# The Back-to-Back Champions

## Doyle Brunson, 1976-77
WSOP Winnings through 2002 — $1,777,959

## Stu Ungar, 1980-81
WSOP Winnings through 1998 — $2,081,478

## Johnny Chan, 1987-88
WSOP Winnings through 2002 — $3,091,494

Johnny Chan began playing poker in nickel-dime games while he was a student at the University of Houston. Not long after becoming a professional poker player, he won the America's Cup at Bob Stupak's Vegas World casino. It was Stupak who nicknamed Chan the "Orient Express." Chan had a remarkable run of success in tournament poker when he won two consecutive WSOP titles in 1987-88 followed by winning the inaugural Hall of Fame tournament in 1988 and capped by his runner-up finish at the WSOP in 1989.

# 1982 World Championship Event
## 13th World Series of Poker
### Number of Entries: 104

———— The Championship Table ————

| The Finalists | Hometown |
|---|---|
| Doyle Brunson | Lubbock, TX |
| Carl Cannon | Mexia, TX |
| Buster Jackson | Texas |
| Berry Johnston | Las Vegas, NV |
| A.J. Meyers | Beverly Hills, CA |
| Sailor Roberts | San Angelo, TX |
| Dody Roach | Stephenville, TX |
| Jack Straus | Austin, TX |
| Dewey Tomko | Haines City, FL |

———————— The Last Hand ————————

**Straus' Cards**  **Tomko's Cards**

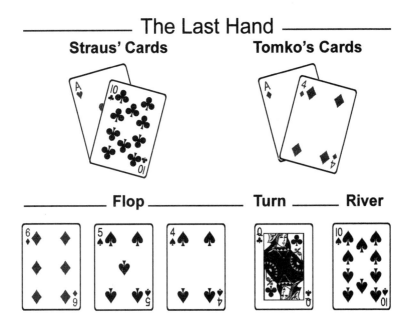

———— Flop ———— Turn ——— River

| The Finish | Prize Money |
|---|---|
| 1st Straus | $520,000 |
| 2nd Tomko | $208,000 |
| 3rd Johnston | $104,000 |
| 4th Brunson | $ 52,000 |
| 5th Meyers | $ 52,000 |
| 6th Roach | $ 41,600 |
| 7th Jackson | $ 20,800 |
| 8th Roberts | $ 20,800 |
| 9th Cannon | $ 20,800 |

## How It Happened

Jack Straus and Dewey Tomko got all their chips into the pot before the flop. A four came on the flop to give Tomko the lead, but the river brought a 10 that won the championship for Straus.

## Highlights

Spectators were standing 25-deep when the final hand was played between Straus and Tomko, the biggest single pot to date in World Series history at $967,000. Earlier in the tournament, Straus had been down to his last $500 chip and made an amazing comeback to victory. The 1982 WSOP finale paid the biggest winnings of any single sports event in the country.

Doyle Brunson became the first player in WSOP history to win $1 million in total prize money in all events over the years. He took third place in the ace-to-five lowball event and fourth in the championship event (his 10th series win) to bring his accumulated winnings to a total of $1,063,875.

Thirteen tournaments were scheduled with 1,253 entrants vying for $2,607,700 in total prize money. Vera Richmond became the first woman to win an open event, the $1,000 ace-to-five draw game. June Field, who founded *Card Player* magazine in 1988, won the ladies championship. Tommy Abdo was inducted posthumously into the Poker Hall of Fame. Several years earlier, he had suffered a heart attack at the poker table, asked someone to count his chips and save his seat until he returned to the game. He died that night.

## Dewey Tomko
### A 1996 Conversation with Dana Smith

When I interviewed Dewey Tomko in 1996, he had just flown into Las Vegas from his home in Haines City, Florida, to play a little poker during the World Series. The former kindergarten teacher was preparing to change  gears, poker parlance for taking a different direction, by abandoning the world of mega-stakes poker to follow his dream of joining the PGA Seniors Tour. As manager of the Southern Dunes Golf and Country Club in Haines City (near Disney World) that he, Jack Binion and Doyle Brunson jointly own, Tomko plays golf every day and decided to take a swing at the Seniors Tour for much the same reason that he once decided to become a professional poker player.

"I was sitting in the $10-$20 game at the Golden Nugget in the early '70s" he explained, "and noticed Jack Binion and those other guys playing high-stakes hold'em. I told a buddy that I wanted to go over and play with them. 'You don't wanna play in that game,' he said. 'They're too good for you.' But I had to try it, that's just the way I am. And that's how I've always been—I need a challenge."

Whether he will be a success playing pro golf is still a question, but there is no question that Tomko is one of the most successful poker players in the world. His latest feat was finishing second, worth a cool $1.1 million, in the 2001 WSOP championship event when his pocket rockets went down in flames on the river card, which made a straight for Carlos Mortensen. "I played as well as I could have," he told newspaper reporters. "Fate is fate."

It wasn't the first time that he has finished second. "We used to have some big tournaments. There was the WSOP, Amarillo Slim's Super Bowl of Poker, and Bob Stupak's big tournament at Vegas World. In 1982 I finished second in all of them! I came in second about fifteen times before I ever won a tournament and it got to be quite a stigma. Then I won a bunch of them."

In fact Tomko has won a lion's share of tournament titles, yet he left full-time gambling in favor of a day job because he was getting burned out on poker. "I've got orange groves and some other investments from poker and so I don't need to play it anymore. Anybody that's in gambling and enjoying it, that's great but I kinda got burned out on it. Jack Binion, who's one of the smartest men I know, told me years ago when I was making money hand over fist at poker, 'You oughta invest this money and do something with it. When you get to be about 45 years old, you might not want to play poker anymore.' At the time I thought he was nuts, but it turned out that he was right, as usual.

"There are two ways to play poker. When you're young, you make as much money as you possibly can and invest it so that you can play poker leisurely. Then if you lose, you've still got plenty of money coming in. Or you could be like Lyle Berman. He started playing poker late, after he had become successful in business. Several businessmen over 45 have done the same thing."

What will Tomko do if his plan to become a pro golfer doesn't work out, I wondered. "I'll try it for a few years and if I feel like I can't compete in it, I'll go back into poker. Most poker players are like athletes. They need competition. The American lifestyle is to compete but in the average job, there's nothing to compete at. So you're searching for something. Most people get into gambling because it's a form of competition."

"I've always questioned myself about whether I should play poker, whether it has socially redeeming qualities. But let me tell you something about life—everybody is gambling! If you're a hardware store guy and you open up a business, you're gambling that somebody will come and buy something. If you're on a paycheck, you're gambling that whoever hired you will keep you on." Tomko's total winnings at the WSOP through 2002 totaled $1,915,644.

"I'm feeling great and ready to play. Only problem is I lost my glasses. Got propositioned from the rail last night and couldn't even read the damn note."
    — Jack Straus to reporter Al Reinert at the 1973 WSOP

"Jack Straus will bet on anything—even a cockroach race!"
    — Puggy Pearson

# 1983 World Championship Event
## 14th World Series of Poker
### Number of Entries: 108

## ———— The Championship Table ————

| The Finalists | Chip Count | Hometown |
|---|---|---|
| Doyle Brunson | $252,500 | Lubbock, TX |
| Robbie Geers | $ 52,500 | Las Vegas, NV |
| George Huber | $ 28,000 | Las Vegas, NV |
| John Jenkins | $ 52,500 | Austin, TX |
| Carl McKelvey | $ 59,000 | San Jose, CA |
| Tom McEvoy | $117,000 | Grand Rapids, MI |
| Donnacha O'Dea | $ 55,000 | London, UK |
| Rod Peate | $389,000 | Newport Beach,CA |
| R.R. Pennington | $ 73,000 | Texas |

## ———— The Last Hand ————

**McEvoy's Cards**  **Peate's Cards**

Flop ———— Turn —— River

| The Finish | Prize Money |
|------------|-------------|
| 1st McEvoy | $540,000 |
| 2nd Peate | $216,000 |
| 3rd Brunson | $108,000 |
| 4th McElvey | $ 54,000 |
| 5th Geers | $ 54,000 |
| 6th O'Dea | $ 43,200 |
| 7th Jenkins | $ 21,600 |
| 8th Pennington | $ 21,600 |
| 9th Huber | $ 21,600 |

## How It Happened
### by Tom McEvoy

We had been playing heads-up for seven hours when the final hand came up. Everybody sensed that the end was near. The blinds were $8,000-$16,000 and Rod raised $40,000 on the button with K-J suited. I hadn't had one big pocket pair all day long and here I was looking down at two queens. 'I'm all in!' I announced. Rod didn't take a lot of time to call, which surprised me. In hindsight, of course, he has regretted his hasty decision, but at the time he was just exhausted. I had been playing to try to wear him down and, basically, that plan had been working.

Rod would have regained the lead if he had been able to draw out on my queens (the pot was over $600,000). When my two queens held up, I jumped up from my seat with my arms raised in victory. Winning the championship was the fulfillment of my dreams, the thrill of my life.

## Highlights

1983 was the first year that a satellite winner won the "big one." In the 1984 World Series of Poker brochure, *Las Vegas Sun* reporter Pete Peters wrote:

> McEvoy and runnerup Peate fulfilled the dream of 'ordinary' poker players. They gained their entry into the main event by virtue of satellite tournaments—McEvoy at the Horseshoe and Peate at the Bingo Palace.
>
> It was at the Bingo Palace where then poker room manager Tom Bowling gave the 'ordinary' player the dream of a lifetime: earning

his way to the Horseshoe's WSOP. Satellite tournaments are the brainchild of WSOP tournament director, Eric Drache. He came up with the idea to give small stakes players and amateurs a chance to compete with the top professionals.

McEvoy's double-win—he also won the limit hold'em tournament—put him in third place in total money won at the Series at that time, behind Doyle Brunson and Stu Ungar. In those days the winner of each WSOP event received 50 percent of the prize pool, in contrast to about 30 percent for the winner of the championship event in 2002, and about 40 percent for the winners of the preliminary events.

With 1,053 entries, the prize money at the '83 WSOP passed the $3 million mark for the first time. Two new tournaments were added to the schedule—limit Omaha high and match play. Road gambler Joe Bernstein was inducted into the Poker Hall of Fame.

## Making the Final "Casino" at the 1983 WSOP
### by Tom McEvoy

In 1983 during the WSOP all the hotel rooms in Downtown Vegas were fully booked and business was booming. The Shoe didn't have its own cardroom at that time—they didn't have one until 1988 when they acquired the Mint, which had an existing cardroom that was simply incorporated into the Shoe. (In fact Jim Albrecht was the cardroom manager at the Mint. You could say that he was in the right place at the right time, as far as his association with the WSOP goes.) Because the Horseshoe didn't have enough space for all of the WSOP action, even though the Series was much smaller then than it is today, they had to use tables from adjacent casinos—the Nugget, Queens and Fremont all had poker rooms. They didn't just borrow tables; some of the tournament games actually were played in the cardrooms of the rival casinos.

We even made jokes about "making the final casino." For example, the limit hold'em tournament had 234 players and since the Shoe didn't have enough space, some of the entrants had to play at the Nugget. As players busted out and a table was broken down, they would be transferred to the Horseshoe and simply carry their chips across the street with them. (I think the tournament officials had walkie-talkies to contact each other.) But for the main event, they squeezed 12 nine-handed tables into the Horseshoe.

Some of the preliminary events were held downstairs in the Sombrero Room, where the coffee shop is located today. They closed the restaurant and put in poker tables, and they took out some slot machines so they could set up a few tables on the main floor. I think the Shoe had a cardroom in the early '70s (in the nook where the baccarat table is today) and Sailor Roberts managed it, but after a while it was closed. So for years, the Horseshoe held the WSOP without having a regular poker room.

Strangely, I can't remember hands that I won last week, but I still remember hands that I played in the championship event. I guess that's because it was such a turning point in my life, certainly the defining moment in my poker career. And I absolutely knew in my heart and soul that I needed to win because I may never get another shot at it. Unfortunately it turns out that I was a prophet. Since 1983, the highest I have placed in the championship event is fortieth, although I have won two more gold bracelets since then. In all I have four bracelets, the two that I won in '83, one for razz in '86, and one for limit Omaha in '92.

At one time, Rod Peate had over $800,000 in chips and I had a little over $200,000. Slowly, I reversed things to the point where I had $780,000 and he had the rest going into the final hand. The blinds had gone up to $8,000-$16,000, which was the record at that time (and one that stood for several years, even though the number of entries increased). One of the reasons why the blinds got that high was because Rod and I played heads-up for seven hours! We actually went into the fifth day: It was 1:45 a.m. on Friday before we finished playing. The television cameramen swore that they would never come back to film the WSOP again—they thought that we were deliberately stalling just to stay in the limelight. That wasn't true at all, of course. I felt that I had to win this tournament and I had a game plan, namely a long slow grind against Rod. In other words, there were plenty of chips in play for the size of the blinds to grind it out. Plus they had given us a two-and-a-half-hour dinner break—apparently, they thought it would be over too quickly because we had been firing at each other earlier. It was around 3:30 in the afternoon when Doyle busted out in third place, so players had been dropping like flies. Maybe they wanted the match to appear on the evening news and they thought it was going to be over too fast, I don't know. But once we got heads-up, I did a reverse by going into a shell. Then when I found myself losing with that strategy, I opened up my game again. The lead seesawed back and forth, and once I got things back to even, I stayed close the rest of the way.

In fact Mike Sexton said that I set poker back at least ten years by this long, drawn-out process because indeed the TV crews did not come back for the next three or four years as the result of what happened in '83. I had warned Jack Binion and some of the other tournament officials. "This is not going to be like the '82 final between Jack Straus and Dewey Tomko," I said, "which lasted for about 10 minutes. They played a million-dollar pot before the flop when the blinds were only $2,000-$4,000!" They put a million dollars in, half a million each, on A-10 offsuit and the A-4 of diamonds, which I thought was ridiculous. That had stuck in my mind, and I knew that I wasn't going to do such a silly thing.

An Irish player who just missed the final table sort of hung close to me (maybe because of my Irish ancestry), watching my play. Earlier he had taken me aside, given me some advice, and built up my confidence. Then during the long dinner break, he gave me a full-body massage, which helped immensely in getting me totally relaxed. I had dinner with my wife and friends and we talked a little bit about the tournament, but mostly I just relaxed.

Bobby Baldwin interviewed me during the break and asked if I had a strategy in mind for the final table. My strategy was rather tight and conservative because I knew that Rod would be coming after me, but when it wasn't successful I changed it and opened up my game. At one time I made a mistake by laying down two pair against Rod when I had 9-7 and he had 10-8. There was a 10-9-7 on board, so I had two pair and he had an open-ended straight draw, top pair, and picked up a flush draw on fourth street. My mistake was that I led $60,000 at the pot and he just went whoosh, all in. I folded. When I bet the $60,000, Rod's all-in raise was forcing me to call all the rest of my chips, whereas if I had checked and he had bet, I could have called a reasonable bet. If I had won, it probably would have been basically over, but if I had lost, I would have been crippled. I had been pushing him a little bit so he was ready to gamble and just took a stand with the hand.

Rod (pictured here in 1983) was very aggressive throughout the final table and continually put pressure on me. My tight-conservative play wasn't working because I wasn't getting enough good cards and he kept hammering away at me. Finally I caught a key hand that turned things around. Rod raised with the 7♣ 6♣, I reraised with K-Q offsuit, taking a stand with the hand, and he called. The flop came queen-high with a couple of clubs, so he flopped a flush draw and then paired one of his cards on the turn, giving him a lot of outs. Rod was way ahead of me in chips at the time, about $800,000 to my $200,000. He didn't get there with his draw and I moved up to about an equal chip position with him. The main reason that I ultimately won the championship is that I never got my money in on a draw, and when my opponents had drawing hands, they never made their draws. I was very fortunate.

I used to play all my cash games ($10-$20) at the Golden Nugget, and many of my colleagues stayed in the gallery throughout the tournament to cheer me on. A lot of them also were rooting for Rod—we were two of "theirs" who got there, two $10-$20 dark-horses that they all could identify with, two of their regular friends who just happened to place first-second in the championship event at the World Series of Poker.

The third-place finisher was the legendary Doyle Brunson, who already had won back-to-back championships in '76-'77. Then in 1980 against the rookie Stu Ungar, he came in second. With the possible exception of Amarillo Slim, Doyle was the most famous poker player in the world. Three-handed Doyle played a hand against Rod Peate and got himself broke. Doyle had the J♦ 9♦ in the small blind. Rod raised on the button with pocket nines. I folded. The flop came nine-high with two diamonds, giving Doyle top pair and a flush draw—which looks pretty good on the surface—but he was up against Rod's set of nines. On the flop he checked and Rod bet about $15,000. Doyle moved all in with over a quarter-million in chips. He overbet the pot, apparently trying to run over Rod, but Rod had made it something like $9,000 before the flop, and $15,000 to go on the flop, so he wasn't about to relinquish the hand. He called Doyle's all-in bet and sent the legend to the rail.

The fourth-place finisher was Carl McKelvey, a road gambler who travels all over the country playing pot-limit and no-limit games wherever he can find them. He plays a few tournaments and always comes to the WSOP primarily to play the pot-limit side games. Carl had practically no chance to finish any higher than fourth because by the time it got down to four-handed, he had only $50,000 in chips while everybody else had $300,000 or more. In fact I was the leader four-handed, but when it got to heads-up Rod had a 3-to-2 chip lead on me after busting Doyle.

Robbie Geers, who finished in fifth place, also had won a Bingo Palace satellite. He got broke when he finally was dealt a pair of kings and decided to slow-play them against Peate, who had suited connectors. Geers flopped a set and Peate flopped a flush draw. Geers checked, Peate moved in on him, and Geers called. Peate made the flush to beat him.

Donn O'Dea, who was the best player in Ireland at the time, finished in sixth place. He was also the runner-up to me in the limit hold'em event a few days before the championship tournament. Interestingly, after he came in second in the limit hold'em event, it took him 17 years to win a gold bracelet (in pot-limit Omaha) at the WSOP. He said that he blamed me for it taking him so long to win!

The seventh place finisher, John "Austin Squatty" Jenkins, was a friend of mine who was murdered in 1989 when he was shot in the back of the head. Jenkins was in the rare book business and was sort of a short fellow who always had a big cigar in his mouth. In his final hand in the tournament, I raised with pocket sixes and he played back at me with A-K. We got it all in. The flop came with an ace and a six in it, so he flopped top pair and I flopped a six to win the pot. Coincidentally, the same type of thing happened over a decade later when Jim Bechtel had pocket sixes against John Bonetti's A-K and knocked Bonetti out in third place.

The eighth-place finisher was R.R. Pennington, a Texan who disappeared from the poker scene soon after that. I was being rather aggressive at the time and raised with K-10 offsuit, a marginal hand. He called with the A♦ 10♦. I flopped a king and Pennington flopped a royal flush draw! I wasn't much of a favorite to him. He check-raised me all in. I thought and thought about it, and finally decided to call. That raised some eyebrows because he had been playing pretty snug for most of the tournament and nobody thought that I possibly could have the best hand. It turned out that I did have the best hand, but I was up against a monster draw. Fortunately for me, Pennington didn't get there, which goes back to what I said earlier: Other players missed their big draws against me and I eliminated them, which gave me enough chips to get off and running.

Las Vegas pro George Huber, who is still playing poker, finished ninth. Huber placed third in the championship event in 1979, the year that Hal Fowler won it. He was pretty short-stacked at the final table and never really had a chance.

I realize how fortunate I was to win, and to make poker history as the first satellite winner. I'll probably spend the rest of my poker career trying to duplicate that win. Many years later, Rod Peate jokingly told me that I had milked more from my WSOP win than any other player in history. While a lot of the other champions have since faded into obscurity, I have built upon my win by expanding my poker career into writing poker books and magazine columns. Since poker has added so much to my life, that's the least I can do to give something back to the world of poker.

"Better one day as a lion than one-hundred years as a lamb."
— Inscription on the pendant that Jack Straus, 1982 World Champion who loved big-game hunting as much as he did poker, wore around his neck. A former basketball player at Texas A&M, where he received a degree in business administration, Straus died in 1988 at the age of 58 after suffering a heart attack during a high-stakes poker game at the Bicycle Club in Southern California.

"God may play dice with the universe, but serious gamblers prefer no-limit Texas hold'em."
                              — Jim McManus in "Positively Fifth Street"

"The World Series of Poker deck will forever be missing one king."
                    — Jack McClelland upon Johnny Moss' death in 1995   **89**

# 1984 World Championship Event
## 15th World Series of Poker
### Number of Entries: 132

## ———— The Championship Table ————

| The Finalists | Chip Count | Hometown |
|---|---|---|
| Mike Allen | $ 38,000 | Kansas City, MO |
| Jesse Alto | $369,000 | Houston, TX |
| Howard "Tahoe" Andrew | $ 27,000 | California |
| David Chew | $121,000 | Lakewood, CO |
| Rick Hamil | $ 74,000 | Unknown |
| Jack Keller | $318,000 | Las Vegas, NV |
| Rusty LePage | $ 59,000 | McAllen, TX |
| Curtis "Iron Man" Skinner | $ 86,000 | Fort Worth, TX |
| Byron "Cowboy" Wolford | $241,000 | Dallas, TX |

## ———— The Last Hand ————

**Keller's Cards**          **Wolford's Cards**

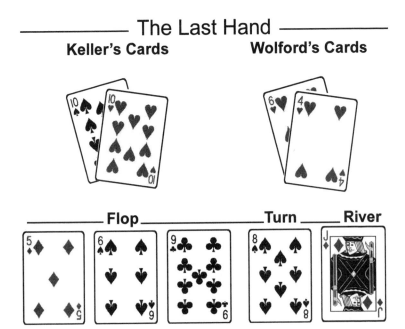

———— Flop ———————— Turn ———— River

| The Finish | Prize Money |
|---|---|
| 1st Keller | $660,000 |
| 2nd Wolford | $264,000 |
| 3rd Alto | $132,000 |
| 4th Chew | $ 66,000 |
| 5th Hamil | $ 66,000 |
| 6th Skinner | $ 52,800 |
| 7th Allen | $ 26,400 |
| 8th Andrew | $ 26,400 |
| 9th LePage | $ 26,400 |

## How It Happened

"I had a lot of outs on the flop, a pair and drawing to a straight if the right cards came," Cowboy Wolford recalled. "But Jack's luck held up and he won the title with a pair of tens." The oddsmakers listed Keller, who had sold his auto body shop in Philadelpia and moved to Las Vegas two years earlier, at 50-to-1 to win the title. "Since I moved here I've mostly been losing the money I made from the sale of my business," Keller told reporters. "I had four steady days of luck, which is what you need to win this one." Earlier Keller had won the seven-card stud event at the Series. His WSOP winnings through 2002 totaled $1,593,645.

A hand that has become a part of poker lore turned the tide in Keller's favor when Wolford successfully bluffed Alto, the chip leader, in a $200,000 pot at the championship table. Apparently on tilt, Alto then threw off all his remaining chips to Keller.

## Highlights

When it got down to three players, the chips were exchanged for cash and $50,000 bundles of bills rolled across the table as Keller, Wolford and Alto bet back and forth. Tournament director Eric Drache stated, "The astounding volume of how-to literature that is a by-product of the boom in poker's popularity has helped narrow the gap between so-called professionals and amateurs. A decade ago probably 75 percent of the people at the World Series were professionals. It's a lot less than that now."

1984 was the first year that pot-limit Omaha was scheduled as a WSOP event. Total prize money was $3,455,000 with 1,537 entries. "Horseshoe President Jack Binion is confident that the 200-entry level in the no-limit hold'em finale will quite likely be passed within the next couple years," the '85 WSOP brochure stated. (It actually took seven years—1991 was the first WSOP championship event with 200 or more entries.) "The big reason for this is the explosion in the popularity of tournament satellites.The WSOP also has helped create marketable poker personalities who proceeded to develop their own successful poker extravaganzas. Amarillo Slim and Jack Straus are examples of such people."

Murph Harrold, widely regarded as one of the best deuce-to-seven draw players of all time, was inducted into the Hall of Fame.

## Byron "Cowboy" Wolford
### Rodeoing 'n Playing Poker
### Interview with a Champ (1999)
### by Dana Smith

Tie your horse to the hitchin' post, amble through the swingin' doors, elbow your way to the poker table in the back of the joint, and plan to set a spell. Cowboy just rode into town and he's got a saddle bag full of stories to tell about the days when he roamed the range rodeoing and playing poker.

Byron "Cowboy" Wolford has won as many titles roping calves in big rodeos as he has playing poker in major tournaments. From the late '40s through 1960 he traveled the rodeo circuit with famous cowboys such as Don McLaughlin and Casey Tibbs. All the while, he was playing poker with his cowboy compadres, running games out of hotel rooms and horse trailers. "I didn't know until now that I was having so much fun. I just thought it was a natural thing that you did back then," he said of that time in his life.

When his rodeo career ended, he turned to poker full-time as a road gambler on the Southern circuit traveled by Doyle Brunson, Bobby Baldwin, Titanic Thompson, T. J. Cloutier and other legendary gamblers who faded the white line from Houston to Dallas to Shreveport. Although he won the $5,000 limit hold'em title at the 1991 World Series of Poker and finished second to Jack Keller in the 1984 championship event, it is his adventures as a champion calf roper that the gifted story teller talked about first.

*You also played a lot of poker during the time that you were a rodeo star.*

Yes. A lot of people have asked me if I've played poker all my life and I answer, "Not yet." We mostly played "wheel" lowball, no-limit poker. We had some big games back then. We stayed at the Belvedere Hotel across the street from Madison Square Garden and our lowball game would never break up, it was a 30-day marathon. If a seat came up at 3:00 in the morning, you'd get a wake-up call to come play. I ran the game and charged 'em $1 an hour to play. Of course I played in it, too. One time when Roy Rogers was the star of the show, the Sons of the Pioneers played in our game and they lost everything but their guitars! I kept telling them, "Why don't y'all bring Roy up here?" We knew he had plenty of money. "No," they said, "he's real religious. Don't tell him we're playin'." They were some of the worst gamblers I've ever seen—I don't know how they sang about the tumblin' weeds at the night shows.

*Lowball must be your favorite game?*

Yes, I won the deuce-to-seven championship in 1979 at Amarillo Slim's Super Bowl of Poker when it had a $10,000 entry fee. Then I split first place money with Bobby Baldwin at the World Series of Poker. I had him down to $15,000 and he made a comeback and broke me. I think I stood pat on a jack and he drew three cards to beat me, and I never won another pot after that.

*You ran a club in Dallas in the old days where a lot of famous gamblers played poker.*

I had a place called the Redman's Club down on Greenville Avenue that I ran for about five years. We had a couple of limit games, but mostly it was no-limit. I had games where there was $200,000 on the table. Bob Brooks, Bobby Baldwin, Everett Goulsby, T. J. Cloutier—a lot of people played there. The cardroom was upstairs. Downstairs was the entry and then there was an iron door where I could buzz them in or out (everybody had to have a membership card). We had a big no-limit game and Hugh Briscoe from Denton, Texas, lost a lot of money in it. Of course, he had a lot of money to lose. In this one game, a fella named Speedy and Mr. Briscoe were in a big hold'em pot together. Mr. Briscoe flopped three jacks and Speedy flopped three fours. Everybody took turns dealing back then and we had a rule that you could cut the cards at any time during the game if you threw $5 into the pot. With one card to come, there was about $30,000 in the pot when Mr. Briscoe threw in $5 and said, "Cut the cards." The dealer cut the cards, burned one, and out came the case four—Speedy made quad fours! That was one of the worse things I've ever seen in a poker game.

*I'll bet he never asked for the cards to be cut again! Were there a lot of guys toting guns in those days?*

No, not too many, but I played in Oklahoma one time when I was the only who didn't have a gun. We mostly played at the Redman's Club right there in downtown Dallas. O. T. Bounds, Titanic Thompson—all these ol' guys I used to know played there. Titanic (we called him "Ty") was quite a character. Back in '60 he said to me, "You're from Tyler—let's open up one of these Redman's clubs down there." So, we got a charter and opened up a club right across from the courthouse in downtown Tyler. Ty was a scratch golfer left or right handed and, in general, a proposition man. Any time it looked like you had the nuts, don't worry, brother—you couldn't win.

*How about Titanic's scam with the "poker psychic?"*

Ty had a deal back then where he'd be sitting around poker places that he'd never been to before and he'd say, "You know, guys, I know this woman who's a psychic. I'll tell you how good she is: You take a card out of that deck and put it on the table in front of us. She doesn't live in this state, but I'll bet you that if you go call her, she'll tell you what the card is." Well, back then there wasn't any TV, no shortwave stuff, and Ty had been right there with them all the time, hadn't gone anywhere. Mighty near anybody would go for that deal. So, he bet $1,000 that they could call this woman who was a psychic and she could tell them over the telephone exactly what that card was. Then somebody would take a card out and put it on the table.

"Okay," he'd say, "here's the long distance number. Just ask for Miss Brown." They'd call and say, "Is Miss Brown there?"

"Just a moment," someone would answer. In a minute another voice said "Hello?"

"Miss Brown, we're down here in so-and-so and we've got a bet on. This gentleman says you're quite a psychic."

"I think I am," she'd say.

"Well, we've taken a card out of the deck and laid it in the middle of the table and he bet that you could tell us what card it is." She'd answer, "Give me a moment." After a short pause, she'd say, "The four of diamonds." And the guy would almost faint. Of course, Ty had a different name for every card in the deck. If it was the four of diamonds, he'd tell them to ask for Miss Brown. If it was the nine of hearts, it might be Miss Ruby.

*Do you miss those days, Cowboy?*

Yeah, I do. I've got a thousand stories and they're all true. Stories about lots of famous ropers and gamblers, one about "Mac" McCorquedale who brought hold'em to Las Vegas. He was playing at Redman's in Dallas and wanted me to go out to Vegas with him but I was too busy doin' nothin'. He was a good player—he's in the Poker Hall of Fame—and he was quite a character. Mac opened up at the California Club when he came out to Vegas and introduced hold'em to everybody. I played in a few of those games, but they had learned pretty good by the time I got there. I was playing out at the Horseshoe, you know, before it had the World Series. They had a no-limit game there one time that lasted nine months and never broke up. There were guys from Louisiana and Texas in it, Sid Wyman who owned the Dunes, and Bernstein, and they were all playing hold'em. They had played in the game at the California Club for a while, but when they first started they'd take two fours and it didn't make any difference what came on the flop, they'd call you. And it was no-limit! They were stud players, you know, and they didn't understand about outs and all that. Sid Wyman would bet $25,000 on a baseball game, a pretty big bet back then.

McCorquedale knew Johnny Moss, who had already been in Vegas for a while, because we had all played no-limit poker together down in Texas. The first time I ever met Moss was in '51. I'd come in from rodeoing and he had a game in Waco. They all liked me because I was a cowboy, I was young and strong and friendly. I used to play $10 limit with Doyle Brunson in Dallas and I met Sailor Roberts in '55 while I was training my horses during the winter. Then when I went out to Vegas, I met Benny and all of 'em. Benny liked cowboys, you know, and he knew cowboys that I rodeoed with and we got to know each other real good.

*I heard that you once lost your horse in a poker game.*

Yes, ma'am, I did. I had this sorrel mare that we called "Glass Eye" because she had a white eye. She could see out of it, it was just a different color than her other one. I'm up in Weiser, Idaho, and got to playing poker with these cowboys from California—they probably had more cards in their boots as they had on the table —and I lost ol' Glass Eye, my roping horse. I started driving back home real slow to get me another horse because I didn't know what I was gonna tell my daddy. When I pulled in the driveway he was out walking under the pecan tree, just like he had been waiting for me. I pulled in, he looked in the trailer, and he didn't say "Son, how you doin'?" or "Glad to see ya"—he said, "Where's ol' Glass Eye?"

"I hate to tell you, Daddy, but I lost her in a poker game."

"Do you mean that you lost that horse in a poker game?!"

"No, I didn't put her up in the middle of the table and bet her," I answered. "I sold her and lost the money."

"Boy, you're a real dandy!" he said and strode off. I'd rather have had him whip me than say that. I didn't want to stay around the house too much, so I took my car and empty trailer the next day and drove down to the San Antonio rodeo. I knew I was liable to run into somebody along the way whose rig was broken down, load his horse up, and we'd hit the rodeo together. Didn't make no difference where we'd go—hell, the world was our oyster back then. So I went there, got in a poker game, and won me a horse.

*You won a horse right after losing one?*

Yep. I won him on three aces and named him Ace. Went back home, pulled in the driveway, and Daddy says, "Where'd you get that ol' gray sonnabitch?"

"Won him in a poker game," I answered.

"It's about time you won one—you've lost enough of 'em," he said. I put ol' Ace up and went out that night, knowin' that by six o'clock in the morning Daddy was gonna get up and by seven he woulda already been ropin' off that horse. He could train a horse better than anybody. So when I came downstairs to have breakfast with my mother, I asked him what he thought of Ace. "I wouldn't give you a quarter for him," he said. "He can't even jerk one down."

"Well, Dad," I said, "I'm going up to Canada and there's a 10-second jerk-down penalty there, so Ace oughta work out fine."

"Well, good luck, but don't call me for money," he answered. I took ol' Ace up there and we won the Canadian championship.

*Your wife Evelyn plays poker—I've seen her name among tournament winners.*

Yes, she's a good player, she was trained by an expert, you know! And Evelyn can sew anything. Did you ever see the Benny Binion dolls that used to be in a display case down by the restaurant in the Horseshoe? She made that pair of dolls to look just like Benny and his wife, made them from scratch, about three feet tall. She put boots on them, made up a pair of glasses for Mrs. Binion's doll, and even put a gold dollar on Benny's shirt. I had a size 4 cowboy hat made in Fort Worth for his doll that cost me $200. It looked just like Benny standing there with Mrs. Binion beside him. Benny loved those dolls, but when the Horseshoe was remodeled somebody just threw them into a back room. I finally went down there and got them, a little messed up. Ten million people looked at those dolls and some folks still ask about them.

*You had a son who worked at the Horseshoe.*

Yes, my boy was named James Alan. When I first took him out to Vegas, Benny said, "Teach him whatever you want to and give him time." He wound up being one of the best hands there. Didn't ever mess with drugs, didn't drink, didn't smoke, didn't gamble, worked all the time. Just before the World Series in 1997 they found him dead in his bed. He was 31 years old and in perfect shape, but he had a rare heart disease that had gone undetected. I was so depressed I couldn't even play in the Series.

*Losing your son makes losing the World Series seem like such a minor thing.*

Yes, it does. But you know, I've won seven seconds and one first in the World Series. I won the $5,000 limit hold'em bracelet in 1991, took second a few years ago in the $1,500 no-limit hold'em;

finished second in deuce-to-seven twice; and won second in the $1,000 hold'em event years ago.

*Tell us about playing with Jack Keller and Jesse Alto at the final table in 1984.*

That's the year I took second in the $10,000 big event. Bobby Baldwin wrote an article about the bluff I pulled on Jesse Alto at the final table. It was me and Jesse and Jack Keller, and Jesse had all the chips. He was just raising every pot, you know. So I decided that on the next hand, I was either gonna get broke or whatever. So I put in $80,000 on a couple of bets to bluff him and then I bet him $200,000 on the end. There was something like two kings and a nine out there and Jesse must've stalled for five minutes—he held 'em, held 'em, held 'em while all the cameras were running. I looked over at my boy and I winked. Finally, Jesse threw his hand in and I showed him my 5-3 offsuit. He went nuts, crazy. I'd known Jesse for a long time, knew how volatile he was. Then he dumped off all his chips to Jack—he had $600,000 and dumped them all off to Jack! So Bobby Baldwin wrote that I won the World Series for Jack Keller, said I pulled off the greatest bluff in Series history.

*Anything you'd like to say to poker players in closing?*

I wish 'em all luck. And don't get too upset—it's just a game, you know! I'll bet I've been broke ten times more than anybody. Of course, I've always maintained that a good poker game is one that you're beatin', no matter what kind of game it is. I'm usually real polite to poker players, you know, but this one guy just kept going on and on and finally I said to him, "Like my daddy told me years ago, I'd rather hear a sucker holler than a pretty gal sing."

"Poker is a game of silent courage and sublimated paranoia."
— Al Reinert in Texas Monthly magazine in 1973

"It's all about competition. Different people are afraid of different things. Me, I'm afraid of embarrassment. If I lose, I don't give a damn about the money, but I just hate the embarrassment of being beaten."          — Jack Straus, 1982 World Champion of Poker

Ten World Series of Poker Champions posed for noted WSOP photographer, Larry Grossman, during the 1995 Series, the last year Johnny Moss (c) played in the WSOP. On Moss' left is Jim Bechtel. Standing (l to r) are Tom McEvoy, Johnny Chan, Stu Ungar, Russ Hamilton, Puggy Pearson, Berry Johnston, Phil Hellmuth and Jack Keller.

# 1985 World Championship Event
## 16th World Series of Poker
### Number of Entries: 140

—————— The Championship Table ——————

| The Finalists | Hometown |
|---|---|
| Jesse Alto | Houston, TX |
| T.J. Cloutier | Richardson, TX |
| Hamid Dastmalchi | England |
| John Fallon | Unknown |
| Berry Johnston | Las Vegas, NV |
| Scott Mayfield | Las Vegas, NV |
| Johnny Moss | Odessa, TX |
| Mark Rose | Texas |
| Bill Smith | Roswell, NM |

————————— The Last Hand —————————

**Smith's Cards**          **Cloutier's Cards**

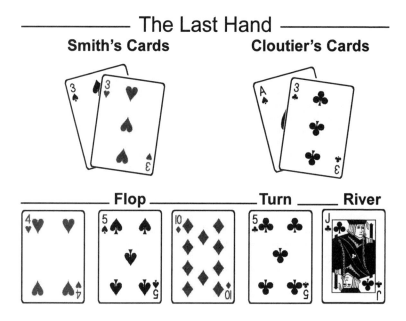

————— Flop ————— Turn ——— River

| The Finish | Prize Money |
|---|---|
| 1st  Smith | $700,000 |
| 2nd Cloutier | $280,000 |
| 3rd Johnston | $140,000 |
| 4th Mayfield | $ 70,000 |
| 5th Dastmalchi | $ 70,000 |
| 6th Alto | $ 42,000 |
| 7th Moss | $ 42,000 |
| 8th Rose | $ 28,000 |
| 9th Fallon | $ 28,000 |

## How It Happened
**by T.J. Cloutier**

I had just won a pot with something like a 5-4 suited, and then I looked down at an ace. Bill raised it and I just moved my stack in. I didn't even look at the second card because there was a chance that I could win it with a raise or if not, I'd probably have the best hand anyway, two overcards if he had a pair. My chances were pretty good. I knew Bill had to make a decision and that if he made the wrong one, I'd be back even with him again. He had started drinking and he gave away money when he was drinking. Bill called my all-in bet and turned over a pair of threes. I looked at my kicker for the first time—it was a three! Now I only had one overcard against his pair. I could have caught an ace or a deuce after the flop to make a straight, but that didn't happen and Bill won the title.

## Highlights

The free buffets that the Horseshoe provided players in the old days during the WSOP were legendary. Restaurant critic Elliot S. Krane described the buffets in 1985: "For one magnificent buffet, Vern Eller prepared a platter of sliced roast pork with a whole, stuffed roast pig displayed in the center of the plate. A giant crab looked down on madallions of crab on a silver platter, while a 12-pound lobster guarded a large dish of the tasty white seafood. On other evenings, buffalo, snake and bear meat were on the menu."

Red Hodges, a noted seven-card stud player, was inducted into the Poker Hall of Fame.

# T.J. Cloutier
## When T.J. Talks, They All Listen
### Interview with a Champ (1999)
### by Dana Smith

If you ask players on the tournament circuit who they think are the best players in the world, T. J. Cloutier's name always comes up. Not because he's won the Big One. He hasn't—yet. But he was the first player to make more than $1 million in prize money without winning the championship event, and he is the all-time leading money winner in tournament poker. Widely regarded as one of the best tournament poker players in the world, Cloutier was the winner of *Card Player* magazine's "Player of the Year" award in 1998 and 2002.

Cloutier won two gold bracelets at the 1994 Series, one for pot-limit hold'em and the other for Omaha high-low. He also has won WSOP titles in limit and pot-limit Omaha. In 1985 he placed second to his long-time friend, Bill Smith, in the championship event, and in 1988 he finished fifth to Johnny Chan at the final table made famous in the movie *Rounders*. Ten years later in 1998 he made his third final-table appearance when he finished third to Scotty Nguyen. However his most famous finish came in 2000 when, starting in last chip position, he finished second to Chris Ferguson, who outdrew Cloutier's better starting hand at the river. (His comments on that event are included in the 2000 WSOP chapter.) Altogether he has won 43 titles in major tournaments, including the $10,000 no-limit hold'em championship at the Bicycle Club's Diamond Jim Brady tournament three years in a row, which many players consider one of the greatest achievements in the history of tournament poker.

T.J. (everybody calls him T.J.) is one of the last of the legendary road gamblers whose numbers are, unfortunately, dwindling each year, taking with them much of the colorful history of poker before it became a commercial commodity. Before he went on the road to make his living playing poker, he played pro football for the Montreal Allouettes, and later owned a wholesale food business with his father and brother in the San Francisco area. When that business closed in 1976 because of an embezzlement by an outside partner, he headed for Texas with $100 in his jeans. "I went to work for six months as a derrick man on the oil rigs. On my off days, I was playing poker. Pretty soon, I was making more money at poker than I was on the rigs—and I'd been freezing up there anyway—so that's how I moved into playing poker full time," he explained. Today T.J., who lives with his wife Joy in Texas, is still a travelin' man, hitting the highways and airways to play major tournaments across the nation. With Tom McEvoy, he is also the co-author of four poker books, including the classic *Championship No-Limit and Pot-Limit Hold'em*. Through 2002, Cloutier had won $2,927,286 at the WSOP.

T.J. is equally well-known as a storyteller. During breaks in the hectic action at the Series, you'll find him surrounded by poker players while he tells his true adventure stories about the gamblers he has played with over the past two decades fading the white line from Dallas to Shreveport to Houston. I listened and laughed as the master of poker tales spun off one yarn after the other from a seemingly endless skeen of memories.

"Little Red Ashey (who's bigger than I am at about 6'5" tall and 300 pounds) and I were staying at the Anthony Motel down in Hot Springs, Arkansas, back in the '70s while we were going to the horse races," T.J. began. 'Let's go next door,' he says. 'Jack Straus is there.' So we start talking with Jack and pretty soon we hear a pounding on the door. Jack opened the door and let a guy in. You had to know Jack to understand this story. He borrowed and loaned a lot of money in his time, and it was always on what we called 'principle.' Principle meant that Jack set up a certain day to pay back his loan, and he only paid it on that exact day.

"Seems that Jack had borrowed $5,000 from this fellow and the guy had come over to dun him for the money. 'I've still got 30 days to pay that off,' Jack said, 'so quit dunning me.' So, the guy left, but as he was going down the stairs, a second man was coming up them. 'I'm down on my luck,' the man tells Jack. 'Could you loan me 10,000?' And Jack peeled the $10 grand right out of his pocket and gave it to him! One time when we were on the golf course, Jack told me that he liked me because I was like him: 'I'm broke one day and have a fortune the next day,' he said. 'And I don't give a damn.'

*You played with some colorful characters in those days.*

Yes I sure did. One of them was George McGann. George loved to play poker, but he was a stone killer. He stood about five feet eight inches tall, and weighed about 145 pounds, and he always wore a suit and tie. Always carried two guns with him, too. One day, George was playing in Dallas and he got broke. So he pulled out his gun and robbed everybody at the game, took every dime they had. "Boys, I'm short," he said. But the kicker to this story is that the very next day, he came back into the game, sat down, and played with these same guys ... and nobody said a word! Some years later, George and his wife were murdered at the same time. The rumor was that he had been collecting money for somebody and they had set him up.

*Tell me about you and Bill Smith.*

He was one of the greatest players of all time, Bill Smith was. He was the tightest player you'd ever played in your life when he was sober. And when he was halfway drunk, he was the best player I'd ever played with. But when he got past that halfway mark, he was the worst player I'd ever played. And you could always tell when he was past the halfway point because he started calling the flop. Say a flop came 7-4-10—he'd say, "21!" When he got up to take a walk, he would have a little hop in his step, a "git-up in his gittalong" we used to call it. And then you knew he was gone. You never worried about Bill when he was sober because you knew that he played A-B-C—tight—and you knew where he was all the time. The only time you worried about him was when he was about halfway drunk, and then he'd play all the way to "H." But he had such great timing on his hands when he was younger and wasn't drunk—he'd make some fabulous plays, plays you couldn't believe. Bill was a truly great player.

*What happened in the 1985 title match at the WSOP?*

When it got to two-handed, I had the lead against Bill, but the key hand of the whole match happened when I had two nines and he had two kings. He moved in and I called him. Bill won the pot and doubled up. Then he had a big lead, and so I started chopping back at him. There were 140 players that year, with $1,400,000 in chips in play, and I got back up to $350,000. Right after that Bill and I played the final hand, which he won with a pocket pair of threes after I had gone all in with an A-3.

*What about your famous "mystery hand?"*

I was playing pot-limit hold'em down in Shreveport. We'd been playing for quite a few hours and there was a lot of money on the table. A hand came up in which I had the stone nuts on fourth street. I had $5,000 in front of me and made a $2,000 bet. Wayne Edmunds was in the game and he had a habit of putting his head down after he called a bet, so that he never saw what was going on anywhere else. As I was making my bet, the dealer grabbed my cards and threw them in the muck. Of course, Wayne didn't see it happen. "What do I do now?!" I was wondering. I have big hands and so I just kept them out in front of me like I was protecting my cards. The dealer burned and then turned the river card. I bet my last $3,000 and Wayne threw his hand away. I won the pot without any cards! Everybody at the table except Wayne saw what had happened, but nobody said a thing.

*You seem to remember everything that's ever happened in the games you've played. Do you keep a book on players?*

No, it's nothing that formal. It's more like pages opening up in a book in my mind. I've been very observant throughout my entire life and I've always had a sort of photographic memory for how people play their hands in certain situations. If you and I had played poker together five years ago, I wouldn't necessarily recall your name today, but I would remember your face and how you played your hands in different spots, your tendencies. I think that knowing your opponents is the most important thing in big-bet poker. To do that, you have to be alert at all times, even when you're not in a hand, because you can learn something valuable. If a wing fell off a gnat at the end of the table, I'd see it.

*Is that how you get a line on the other players?*

The main thing is being very observant and watching what players do in different situations. A fella who used to play with us in Texas years ago would play as good a poker game as anybody I'd ever seen play—for the first two hours. Then he'd hit a stone wall and his whole game would revert back to the way he always played. You could've put a stop watch on him. He'd start bluffing in bad spots and would start giving his money away. With a player like that, you know that he's going to crumble in two hours, so you just wait him out and win the money.

*You call that kind of knowledge "being the recipient of their generosity." How so?*

We're just like leopards—we can't change our spots. For example, I know a player who always brings it in for a small raise when everybody has passed to him on the button; he never comes in flat. But he's also a good enough player that he doesn't stand a reraise unless he has a big hand. Knowing how he plays the button, you can make a lot of money off this man when you're in the blinds by just popping him back three or four times in a session.

*How important is luck in poker?*

It's not as big a factor as novice players think it is. Speaking of luck, I'll tell you about the unluckiest player in the world. There was this big card game years ago in a house down in Odessa or Midland, don't remember which. Nobody except a few notorious men from the area could play in that game, and they were all what we called "packing" in Texas, they were armed.

Seems that one guy accused another one of cheating (which they were all doing) and the guns started blazing. Two men were killed right there in the game and another guy was shot going out the front door. All of the houses were right next to each other, and the people next door heard all the gun shots and called for the cops. So the man that was shot in the doorway started pounding on the neighbors' door to ask for help, standing there just bleeding to death. The guy opened up the door and killed him with a shotgun, thinking that he was trying to break in. Next time you think you're having an unlucky day in poker, just think about this guy!

"If I get drunk, go broke, and ask to borrow $100 from you, do me a favor. Don't let me have it ... just give me $50."
— Bill Smith to Susie Isaacs at the
Gold Coast Casino in the '90s

Sailor Roberts (to left of dealer), Crandall Addington, Howard "Tahoe" Andrew and Doyle Brunson at the 1976 World Series of Poker. Twenty-two players entered the winner-take-all championship event to make a prize pool of $22,000, won by Doyle Brunson. Brunson successfully defended his title in 1977 and is one of only three men who have won back-to-back world poker championships.

John Bonetti (l to r), Mansour Matloubi, Thomas Chung, Glenn Cozen, Jim Bechtel and Mick Cowley at the championship table of the 1993 World Series of Poker. Holding the microphone is Jack McClelland. The Gallery of Champions hangs in the background.

# 1986 World Championship Event
## 17th World Series of Poker
### Number of Entries: 141

─────── The Championship Table ───────

| The Finalists | Hometown |
|---|---|
| Jesse Alto | Houston, TX |
| Bones Berland | Las Vegas, NV |
| Jim Doman | Las Vegas, NV |
| Mike Harthcock | Winter Haven, FL |
| Tom Jacobs | Denver, CO |
| Berry Johnston | Las Vegas, NV |
| Steve Lott | Victoria, TX |
| Roger Moore | Eastman, GA |
| Bill Smith | Dallas, TX |

─────────── The Last Hand ───────────

**Johnston's Cards**          **Harthcock's Cards**

( No record of the board cards for 1986 could be found.)

"Why would I want to beat all of these donkeys, have all of the chips in front of me, and win only 40 percent of the prize pool?"
— Puggy Pearson to Jeff Shulman in 2003 on why, in addition to a lack of endurance, he no longer plays tournaments

| The Finish | Prize Money |
|---|---|
| 1st Johnston | $570,000 |
| 2nd Harthcock | $228,000 |
| 3rd Berland | $114,000 |
| 4th Alto | $ 62,700 |
| 5th Smith | $ 51,300 |
| 6th Moore | $ 39,900 |
| 7th Lott | $ 34,200 |
| 8th Doman | $ 22,800 |
| 9th Jacobs | $ 17,100 |

## How It Happened
### by Berry Johnston

I raised $20,000 before the flop with an A-10. Mike reraised $100,000. I almost threw the hand away. I had three-fourths of the chips, and if I lost the hand Mike and I would be about even in chips. I decided to go for it and moved all my chips into the center. Mike called all-in. No help came on the board for either of us, so I won the hand with ace-high and a better kicker than Mike had. It was the thrill of my life.

## Highlights

Alabama road gambler Henry Green was inducted into the Poker Hall of Fame. Only eight preliminary tournaments were played prior to the championship event, in contrast to thirteen in 1985.

"To many of my fellow poker players and me, the worst poker day of our poker year is the day when we are eliminated from the WSOP championship event."                                      — Phil Hellmuth

"My first year as a professional gambler was the worst experience I ever had in my life. I borrowed money from friends, ran up my credit cards, and hocked all my jewelry at the pawn shops."
                                                              — Johnny Chan

# 1987 World Championship Event
## 18th World Series of Poker
### Number of Entries: 152

─────── The Championship Table ───────

| The Finalists | Chip Count | Hometown |
|---|---|---|
| Mickey Appleman | Finished 8th | New York, NY |
| Johnny Chan | $461,000 | Las Vegas, NV |
| Bob Ciaffone | $147,000 | Saginaw, MI |
| Eldon Elias | Finished 7th | Palo Alto, CA |
| Dan Harrington | $213,000 | Las Vegas, NV |
| Frank Henderson | $215,000 | Houston, TX |
| Jack Keller | Finished 9th | Lake Cormorant, MS |
| Howard Lederer | $151,000 | Las Vegas, NV |
| Jim Spain | $334,000 | Columbus, MS |

───────── The Last Hand ─────────

Chan's Cards          Henderson's Cards

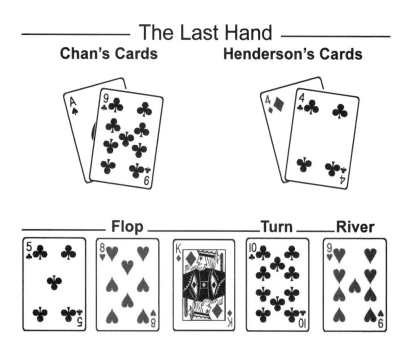

Flop ──────────── Turn ──── River

| The Finish | Prize Money |
|---|---|
| 1st Chan | $655,000 |
| 2nd Henderson | $250,000 |
| 3rd Ciaffone | $125,000 |
| 4th Spain | $ 68,750 |
| 5th Lederer | $ 56,250 |
| 6th Harrington | $ 43,750 |
| 7th Elias | $ 35,500 |
| 8th Appleman | $ 25,000 |
| 9th Keller | $ 18,750 |

## How It Happened

"Chan bet $60,000 before the flop with the A♠ 9♣. I called the $60,000 and raised $240,000 all-in with two fours. The two fours were good until the river when the 9♥ slipped off. This turned out to be the last hand of the tournament." — Frank Henderson

## Highlights

Formerly from Houston, Johnny Chan had played with Frank Henderson in private games in Texas. Chan's nickname was "The Orient Express" and he was in his twenties; Henderson was in his fifties. "My secret was to play slow, play tight, and wait for good hands," Chan said. When only 24 players were left, Henderson was in last place in the chip count.

Thirteen years later in 2000, Chris Ferguson also won the champion event with the A♠ 9♣. Howard Lederer, 23 years old, was the youngest player ever to make the final table at that time. Eleven preliminary events were played, three more than in 1986. 1973 World Champion of Poker Puggy Pearson was inducted into the Poker Hall of Fame.

"I became the first person in poker history to lose a pot with more than a million dollars in it. There are some distinctions that one would rather not have, just ask General George Custer when you get to the hereafter."

— Bob Ciaffone on losing a key hand to Johnny Chan
at the WSOP championship table in 1987

# 1988 World Championship Event
## 19th World Series of Poker
### Number of Entries: 167

————— The Championship Table —————

| The Finalists | Chip Count | Hometown |
|---|---|---|
| Jesse Alto | Finished 9th | Houston, TX |
| Jim Bechtel | $279,000 | Coolidge, AZ |
| Humberto Brenes | $155,000 | San Jose, Costa Rica |
| Johnny Chan | $529,000 | Las Vegas, NV |
| T.J. Cloutier | $431,000 | Richardson, TX |
| Mike Cox | Finished 8th | Unknown |
| Ron Graham | $146,000 | Las Vegas, NV |
| Quinton Nixon | Finished 7th | Charlotte, TX |
| Erik Seidel | $131,000 | New York, NY |

————————— The Last Hand —————————

Chan's Cards       Seidel's Cards

————— Flop ————— Turn ——— River

| The Finish | Prize Money |
|---|---|
| 1st Chan | $700,000 |
| 2nd Seidel | $280,000 |
| 3rd Graham | $140,000 |
| 4th Brenes | $ 77,000 |
| 5th Cloutier | $ 63,000 |
| 6th Bechtel | $ 49,000 |
| 7th Nixon | $ 42,000 |
| 8th Cox | $ 28,000 |
| 9th Alto | $ 21,000 |

## How It Happened

The 1988 championship event has become a classic in World Series of Poker history, in part because Johnny Chan won it for the second consecutive year, and because the final hand that he played against runner-up Erik Seidel was featured in the 1998 movie, "Rounders," starring Matt Damon as a frustrated college student who travels to Las Vegas to play in the "biggest game in town."

When the final hand began, defending World Champion Chan had $1,374,000 in chips and challenger Seidel had $296,000. They both entered the pot for the minimum bet. The flop gave Chan the nut straight and Seidel a pair of queens. Chan bet a modest $40,000. Not suspecting a trap and playing beyond his experience to get this far in the tournament, Seidel raised $50,000 with top pair. The crafty Chan flat-called. The turn card was an innocuous deuce. Chan checked his unbeatable hand. Deceived by Chan's underbet on the flop and his check on the turn, Seidel pushed in all of his remaining chips. The impotent river card changed nothing, and Chan won the World Championship for the second year in a row.

## Highlights

The Binions bought the adjoining Mint Hotel and Casino in 1988, giving the Horseshoe enough space for a permanent poker room. "Binion's Horseshoe has become an establishment in the league of Caesars Palace and Bally's in terms of casino space," the 1989 WSOP magazine proclaimed. "The Horseshoe has long been a tourist attraction in part because of the $1 million in $10,000 bills displayed in the casino and also because it's the home of the World Series of Poker." The tournament area tripled in size the next year. The million-dollar display did not fare quite as well—it was sold after the casino changed hands in 1998.

Two-time World Champion of Poker, Doyle Brunson, author of *Super/System*, was inducted into the Poker Hall of Fame along with the 1982 World Champion of Poker, Jack "Treetop" Straus.

## Erik Seidel
### A 2001 Conversation with Dana Smith

A professional backgammon player as a teenager and a pro poker player by age 28, Erik Seidel was born in Manhattan where he attended Brooklyn College. He also has had a third occupation as a Wall Street trader. His total winnings at the WSOP through 2002 totaled $2,084,161. We began by talking about backgammon in a relaxed and insightful interview dotted by his keen sense of humor, innate honesty and warm personality.

"I started making my living at backgammon at age 17 and got involved with poker through it," Seidel began. "I knew a couple of high-limit poker players in Vegas and in 1985 while I was there for a backgammon tournament, I thought that maybe I should give poker a try. I began by playing $1-$2 limits and somehow I won, which was incredible because I was ridiculously bad. I returned home with the 'bug' and started playing poker with some of the guys that I knew at the Mayfair Club, Steve Zolotow and Bob Beinish. We played for very small stakes, using backgammon chips. But after a while, I took a hiatus from gambling and went to work."

*Mercy, are we talking about a 9-to-5 routine?*

Yes. I had a couple of friends who were working at Paine Webber and thought that I might have the right skills to be a trader. I was lucky in that they put a lot of trust in me right away and within three months, I was trading. Then came the crash of 1987 and I was out of work. That's when I began playing poker much more seriously. By late 1987 I was doing very well and received some encouragement from a couple of the players in the game that

I should go to Vegas to play in the *WSOP.* So I came out in 1988 and played nine single-table satellites going zero for nine. And I played one preliminary no-limit hold'em event plus the championship tournament, in which I came second to Johnny Chan.

*In the movie Rounders, Matt Damon's character watched a video tape of you and Chan dueling at the final table. It's hard to believe it was only the second tournament that you'd ever played. Did you feel intimidated playing Chan?*

Now the truth can be told! It was surreal to find myself heads-up with him at the final table. I was pretty bad in those days, especially shorthanded. I really didn't know what I was doing because I was accustomed to playing in a full 11-handed game so I was trying to figure it out while I was playing him but I wasn't very successful at it. I probably had a combination of good instincts and good luck, but once it got to just the two of us, I didn't have any feel as to how I should be playing the structure or the relative hand values heads up. I remember looking at the whole scene, the lights and cameras and all those chips, and thinking, "What in the world am I doing here, playing heads-up for the world championship?!"

It was pretty awful to be in such a great spot and to be so unprepared for it. Still it was the most incredible experience—to play for four days and get heads-up with Chan—just knowing that I could do it, that I could play at that level. In some ways it was the most awful tournament that I've had because I played so badly heads-up, yet it also was the most exhilarating. I left that tournament with the feeling that I could play at the highest levels. Although I still was very raw, I had learned a lot during that whole event and I didn't feel like I was that far removed from the people who were considered to be the best.

*A few months later, you faced another awesome player heads-up at the Bicycle Club's $2,500 no-limit hold'em event.*

Yes, the brash, young Phil Hellmuth. At that time I didn't know him, no one knew him, but I could see right away that he was an excellent player—plus, he told me so himself. During the break, Phil introduced himself and that night we found ourselves heads-up at the final table. I won the tournament, and the next day Phil won the $5,000 no-limit event. *(The next year, Hellmuth won the championship event against Chan, who was trying for his third straight victory.)*

# 1989 World Championship Event
## 20th World Series of Poker
### Number of Entries: 178

─────── The Championship Table ───────

| The Finalists | Chip Count | Hometown |
|---|---|---|
| Lyle Berman | $185,000 | Minneapolis, MN |
| Johnny Chan | $350,000 | Houston, TX |
| Fernando Fisdel | Finished 7th | New York, NY |
| Noel Furlong | $302,000 | Clifton Lodge, Ireland |
| George Hardie | Finished 9th | Bell Gardens, CA |
| Phil Hellmuth | $344,000 | Madison, WI |
| Steve Lott | $413,000 | Victoria, TX |
| Mike Picow | Finished 8th | Las Vegas, NV |
| Don Zewin | $188,000 | Niagara Falls, NY |

─────── The Last Hand ───────

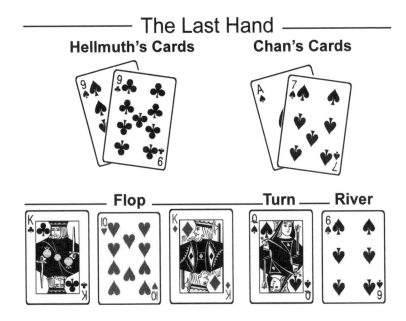

**Hellmuth's Cards**

**Chan's Cards**

─── Flop ─── Turn ── River

| The Finish | Prize Money |
|------------|-------------|
| 1st Hellmuth | $755,000 |
| 2nd Chan | $302,000 |
| 3rd Zewin | $151,000 |
| 4th Lott | $ 83,050 |
| 5th Berman | $ 67,950 |
| 6th Furlong | $ 52,850 |
| 7th Fisdel | $ 45,300 |
| 8th Picow | $ 30,200 |
| 9th Hardie | $ 22,650 |

## How It Happened
### by Phil Hellmuth

I was playing heads-up no-limit hold'em against the two-time reigning World Champion Johnny Chan. The blinds were $5,000-$10,000 and the ante was $2,000 a man. I was on the button and, therefore, had the small blind. My hole cards were the 9♠ 9♣. I opened for $35,000. Chan called the bet and raised $130,000 more. In an instant, I reraised $1 million. After a long deliberation, Chan called $450,000 of my raise with all of his remaining chips. The crowd leapt to its feet as Chan slowly moved his mountain of chips into the middle of the pot. Then we flipped our hands face up. Chan had the A♠ 7♠. This was it! My dream of winning the world championship of poker all came down to one hand.

The flop was K-K-10. All Chan needed was an ace or a 10. The turn card was the Q♠. Chan now needed an ace, 10, jack or queen. I was roughly a 2.5-to-1 favorite. The biggest dream that I had yet dared dream all came down to one card. The last card was the 6♠. My arms shot up into the air—I had achieved my dream!

## Highlights

At the age of 24, Phil Hellmuth became the youngest man ever to win the WSOP championship when he edged out Johnny Chan.

Freddy "Sarge" Ferris was inducted into the Poker Hall of Fame. He gained notoriety in 1983 when the IRS seized $46,000 in chips from him while he was playing a high-stakes cash game during the WSOP.

# 1990 World Championship Event
## 21st World Series of Poker
### Number of Entries: 194

## ———— The Championship Table ————

| The Finalists | Hometown |
|---|---|
| John Bonetti | Houston, TX |
| Dave Crunkleton | Gastonia, NC |
| Berry Johnston | Las Vegas, NV |
| Al Krux | Syracuse, NY |
| Hans "Tuna" Lund | Reno, NV |
| Mansour Matloubi | Cardiff, Wales |
| Rod Peate | Long Beach, CA |
| Stu Ungar | New York, NY |
| Jim Ward | Anchorage, AK |

## ———————— The Last Hand ————————

**Matloubi's Cards**          **Lund's Cards**

———— Flop ———————— Turn —— River

| The Finish | Prize Money |
|---|---|
| 1st Matloubi | $895,000 |
| 2nd Lund | $334,000 |
| 3rd Crunkleton | $167,000 |
| 4th Ward | $ 91,850 |
| 5th Johnston | $ 75,150 |
| 6th Krux | $ 58,450 |
| 7th Peate | $ 50,100 |
| 8th Bonetti | $ 33,400 |
| 9th Ungar | $ 25,050 |

## How It Happened
### by Tom McEvoy

In 1990 Mansour Matloubi faced off against Hans "Tuna" Lund heads-up at the championship table. The blinds were quite high, $15,000-$30,000. On the button Lund went all in with pocket fours for about $300,000. Matloubi called with pocket sixes, so the pot had close to $700,000 in chips in it. Matloubi had a substantial chip lead, so Lund definitely was in trouble going into this hand. If Lund had won this hand, he would have been back in contention for the title. Although he still would have been trailing in the chip count, at least he would have been competitive. The flop came 8-Q-2 with no help for either player on the turn and river. Matloubi won the championship with a pair of sixes.

The highlight of the matchup between Matloubi and Lund, however, was not the final hand, it was a hand that occurred shortly before the showdown. On the button, Mansour brought in the pot for a $75,000 raise with 10♦ 10♣. Lund, who was in the chip lead, called the raise with A♣ 9♦. The flop came 9♠ 2♣ 4♠, giving Lund top pair and top kicker and Matloubi an overpair to the flop. Lund checked, Matloubi led off with a $100,000 bet, Tuna raised $250,000 more. Matloubi studied and thought and called the $250,000 raise and raised the rest of his chips, $378,000. It was Lund's turn to study and think. Finally he shrugged his shoulders and called the raise. I think Lund knew he was beaten at this point, but he had so much money out there he just decided to go for it. In one of the most dramatic hands in WSOP history, the A♠ hit on the turn, giving Tuna the lead with two pair, aces and nines, against Mansour's two tens. Which means that Matloubi had only two outs to win the pot—the two tens left in the deck—which was a 22-to-1 shot. There were 44 unseen cards. Two of them would give Mansour the winning hand and 42 were losers for him. He was in a world of hurt. When the ace hit on fourth street, Mansour was pacing around nervously and actually kicked his chair. With all the money in, Lund has Matloubi covered and will become the world champion unless a two-out 10 falls on the river. And that is exactly what occurred! The miracle 10♠ hit at the river. Mansour won the pot, which had over 80 percent of the chips in it, and went from elimination in second place to the chip lead and the eventual title. Tuna sat motionless and mute, crestfallen over the loss of the hand. Indeed it was a rags to riches hand for Mansour.

One of the most dramatic flip-flop hands in WSOP history, this key hand changed the momentum of the tournament. Of course Lund probably would not have gone broke with fours on the final hand if he had not been forced to play a hand—the blinds were so high that he had to take a stand with something.

## Highlights

1990 was the first year that Omaha high-low split was added to the WSOP schedule. Benny Binion, owner of the Horseshoe and founder of the WSOP, was inducted into the Poker Hall of Fame. Binion died on Christmas day, 1989.

## Hans "Tuna" Lund
### A 1996 Conversation with Dana Smith

When Tuna Lund and I talked in 1996, the agony of the defeat he suffered during the 1990 World Series of Poker was still fresh in his mind. I asked him about the scene in the videotape that showed him losing a gigantic pot to Matloubi just prior to the final hand. "That video did me a great injustice," he said. "It shows me losing a $1,600,000 pot— in the very next hand, it shows me going broke.

What it didn't show is that we played for almost four hours after I lost that big pot, and during that time I made a comeback to $950,000 in chips. Then I slid back down to $300,000, with a lot of fighting in the middle. It was a long, hard battle."

A good battle is something that Lund understands: "It's a real challenge to play against the best players in the world. When I'm playing at the top of my game and they're playing at the top of theirs and the cards are breaking about even, we meet at the final table. Then it's like a life-and-death struggle. To me, the game of poker is not poker—it's a game of war. It's like a conquest with two opposing armies of the same size, and you're the general on both sides. You're looking in the mirror and you have to play against yourself to  see how good you really are. My chips are my troops and I always try to protect them if I can. In some cases I'll stick some out and I'll lose some men. Sometimes I'll lose the whole army, but I always try to choose the best tactics to protect my men."

How do you handle things when you lose a battle, I asked the 6'5" gentle giant. "I suffer. It hurts me to know that I'm playing well but the cards are saying no to me, and so I'm not going to have a chance to win."

Coming that close to winning the title and all that money—how did that feel? "The money meant nothing to me. It's not that I don't want the money, it's that the title means so much more to me. How often in a person's lifetime can he reach his life's dream? How many people ever achieve what they really want to do? My goal is to win the WSOP. The good part is that I came so close. The bad part is that if I'd won the title, I may have retired from poker. After you've achieved your life's ambition, you have to set an even higher goal—and I cannot go any higher than winning the World Series."

"When I got to the final table, I thought that I had made it as far as I could. I was surprised when I won the championship. I entered hoping to get a piece of the pie, and I got it all."

— Mansour Matloubi

# 1991 World Championship Event
## 22nd World Series of Poker
### Number of Entries: 215

## ———— The Championship Table ————

| The Finalists | Chip Count | Hometown |
|---|---|---|
| Brad Daugherty | $150,000 | Reno, NV |
| Ali Farsai | $129,000 | Reno, NV |
| Perry Green | $522,000 | Anchorage, AK |
| Don Holt | $461,000 | Henderson, NV |
| Dan Hunsucker | Finished 8th | Houston, TX |
| Donnacha O'Dea | Finished 9th | London, UK |
| Hilbert Shirey | Finished 7th | Winter Haven, FL |
| Robert Veltri | $541,000 | Los Angeles, CA |
| Don Williams | $330,000 | Las Vegas, NV |

## ———————— The Last Hand ————————

**Daugherty's Cards**          **Holt's Cards**

**———— Flop ————  Turn —— River**

| The Finish | Prize Money |
|---|---|
| 1st Daugherty | $1,000,000 |
| 2nd Holt | $ 402,000 |
| 3rd Veltri | $ 201,250 |
| 4th Williams | $ 115,000 |
| 5th Green | $ 69,000 |
| 6th Farsai | $ 34,500 |
| 7th Shirey | $ 28,750 |
| 8th Hunsucker | $ 23,000 |
| 9th O'Dea | $ 17,250 |

## How It Happened
### by Tom McEvoy

Daugherty had played a key hand earlier in the action in which he won a $1 million pot against Holt, who had the chip lead at the time. That key hand brought the chip count close to even and switched the momentum in Daugherty's favor. As often happens, the play of one hand sets the stage for subsequent hands.

In the final hand, Holt limped on the button with 7-3 and Daugherty raised $75,000 more with K-J. Holt made a minor mistake by limping on the button, but it wasn't terrible because it only cost him half a bet and he had position. But calling the raise was a big mistake. The flop cards were 8-9-J with one heart, giving Holt a three-flush and a gut-shot straight draw (a 10 would make a straight for him). Of course, if Daugherty had a queen in his hand, the 10 would give him an even higher straight. It is dangerous to bluff at coordinated flops because people often will catch a part of it, especially when cards like J-10 or 10-9 come on the flop. That is exactly what happened in the final hand in 1991.

Daugherty checked the flop and Holt moved in for about $450,000. Here they were playing another million-dollar pot! But this time Daugherty had the chip lead going in and he didn't take much time to call Holt's semi-bluff. The 5♣ on the turn gave Holt eight outs to hit a straight, a 6 or a 10. But when the 8♠ came at the river, his drawing days were over and Daugherty became the 1991 world champion—and the first million-dollar winner at the World Series of Poker. Daugherty's winnings at the WSOP through 2002 totaled $1,121,889.

## Highlights

Chris Marlowe narrated this tape along with Chip Reese. Johnny Moss was 84 years old then. This was the first year that the top prize was $1 million because for the first time, there were 200+ entries. Telly Savalas and Gabe Kaplan both played the tournament, and Telly Savalas congratulated Brad for his win. Brunson, Preston, Hellmuth and Ungar all went out on the first day of the tournament.

David Edward "Chip" Reese became the youngest man ever to be inducted into the Poker Hall of Fame. The Dartmouth graduate is regarded by many to be the best all-around high-stakes poker

"He arrived at the Horseshoe on a skateboard." — Anonymous comment by a bystander when Phil Hellmuth won the 1989 World Series of Poker championship at age 24. His winnings at the WSOP through 2002 totaled $2,865,490.

The championship table at the 1990 World Series of Poker. Clockwise from the dealer's left: Hans "Tuna" Lund, Dave Crunkleton, Al Krux, John Bonetti, Mansour Matloubi, Rod Peate, Jim Ward, Berry Johnston and Stu Ungar. 194 players entered the tournament, won by Matloubi whose WSOP winning through 2002 totaled $1,223,432.

Dr. Bruce Van Horn (left), Huck Seed and John Bonetti in three-way action at the championship table of the 1996 World Series of poker. 295 players vied for the $1 million first-place prize money, won by Seed whose total WSOP winnings through 2002 were $1,772,464.

# 1992 World Championship Event
## 23rd World Series of Poker
### Number of Entries: 201

—————— The Championship Table ——————

| The Finalists | Chip Count | Hometown |
|---|---|---|
| Mike Alsaadi | $444,000 | Las Vegas, NV |
| Johnny Chan | Finished 7th | Las Vegas, NV |
| Clyde Coleman | $ 84,000 | Marlowe, OK |
| Dave Crunkelton | $161,000 | Gastonia, NC |
| Hamid Dastmalchi | $751,000 | San Diego, CA |
| Christopher Goulding | Finished 9th | Unknown |
| Tom Jacobs | $246,000 | Denver, CO |
| Jack Keller | Finished 8th | Lake Cormorant, MS |
| Hans "Tuna" Lund | $333,000 | Reno, NV |

————————— The Last Hand —————————

**Dastmalchi's Cards**    **Jacobs' Cards**

———— Flop ———————— Turn ——— River

## The Finish / Prize Money

| The Finish | Prize Money |
|---|---|
| 1st Dastmalchi | $ 1,000,000 |
| 2nd Jacobs | $ 353,500 |
| 3rd Lund | $ 176,500 |
| 4th Alsaadi | $ 101,000 |
| 5th Crunkleton | $ · 60,600 |
| 6th Coleman | $ 30,300 |
| 7th Chan | $ 25,250 |
| 8th Keller | $ 20,200 |
| 9th Goulding | $ 15,150 |

## How It Happened

Dastmalchi began the final-table play with $751,000 in chips, over $300,000 more than the player in second place. Although Dastmalchi had a huge lead when the championship table began, the sentimental favorite to win the title was Hans "Tuna" Lund, who had come so close to victory in the past. Side bets were flowing with Lund supporters chanting his name. To their dismay, Lund went out third leaving Tom Jacobs to vie for Dastmalchi's mountain of chips.

In the final hand Jacobs flopped top two pair and underbet the pot, apparently hoping to win a much larger pot and improve his chip position by allowing Dastmalchi to pay a relatively cheap price to see the turn card. Dastmalchi pondered at length, finally making the call. His dream card 6♥ came on the turn to complete his inside-straight draw. When Dastmalchi checked the nuts, Jacobs moved all in and Dastmalchi called. The river card helped neither player. After a wire-to-wire lead, Dastmalchi became the 1992 World Champion of Poker. His total winnings at the World Series of Poker through 2002 were $1,600,700.

## Highlights

Amarillo Slim Preston was inducted into the Poker Hall of Fame at age 62, twenty years after he won the World Championship of Poker in 1972. Recognized as bringing poker into the national limelight, Preston was still placing high at the WSOP as late as 2000 when he took second place to Philip Ivey in the pot-limit Omaha event. The total prize money for all 20 events in 1992 was $7,769,000.

# 1993 World Championship Event
## 24th World Series of Poker
### Number of Entries: 220

──────── The Championship Table ────────

| The Finalists | Chip Count | Hometown |
|---|---|---|
| Jim Bechtel | $631,000 | Coolidge, AZ |
| John Bonetti | $913,000 | Houston, TX |
| Thomas Chung | $146,000 | Seattle, WA |
| Mick Cowley | $160,000 | Barnsley, England |
| Glen Cozen | $215,000 | Sherman Oaks, CA |
| Brad Daugherty | Finished 9th | Las Vegas, NV |
| Al Korsin | Finished 8th | Las Vegas, NV |
| Thomas Kreilein | Finished 7th | Duncan, Canada |
| Mansour Matloubi | $138,000 | Cardiff, Wales |

──────────── The Last Hand ────────────

**Bechtel's Cards**          **Cozen's Cards**

**Flop** _____ **Turn** ___ **River**

| The Finish | Prize Money |
|---|---|
| 1st Bechtel | $1,000,000 |
| 2nd Cozen | $ 420,000 |
| 3rd Bonetti | $ 210,000 |
| 4th Matloubi | $ 120,000 |
| 5th Chung | $ 72,000 |
| 6th Cowley | $ 36,000 |
| 7th Kreilein | $ 31,200 |
| 8th Korsin | $ 27,600 |
| 9th Daugherty | $ 24,000 |

## How It Happened

Just three deals before the final hand came down, Jim Bechtel and third-place finisher John Bonetti played one of the most widely discussed hands in WSOP history—a hand that far overshadowed the showdown between Bechtel and runner-up Glen Cozen, which seemed anticlimactic after the dramatic hand that preceded it.

In the key hand Bechtel was dealt pocket sixes and bet before the flop. Bonetti and Cozen called . The flop came K-6-4 with two spades. Holding A-K (top pair and top kicker), Bonetti checked on the flop with the intent of check-raising if either of his opponents bet the pot. Cozen also checked. Bechtel bet, Bonetti raised, Cozen folded, and Bechtel flat-called. When the J♠ fell on the turn, Bonetti moved all in and Bechtel called. Bechtel's trip sixes won the pot and raced Bonetti out of the tournament in third place.

The end came swiftly. The blinds were $5,000-$10,000 with a $2,000 ante giving Cozen little room to breathe. On the third deal he went all in with a 7-4. Bechtel called and the rest is history. A cotton farmer and the president of Pinal Gypsum Company in Arizona, Bechtel added $1 million to his corporate wealth and a WSOP bracelet to his wrist. Bechtel's WSOP winnings through 2002 totaled $1,228,745. Bonetti's total was $1,523,532.

## Highlights

Jack Keller, the 1984 World Champion of Poker, was inducted into the Poker Hall of Fame.

# 1994 World Championship Event
## 25th World Series of Poker
### Number of Entries: 268

——— The Championship Table ———

| The Finalists | Chip Count | Hometown |
|---|---|---|
| John Aglialoro | Finished 7th | Haddonfield, NJ |
| Vince Burgio | $550,000 | West Hills, CA |
| Russ Hamilton | $231,000 | Las Vegas, NV |
| Al Krux | $ 91,000 | Syracuse, NY |
| Steve Lott | Finished 9th | Downey, CA |
| Don "Pilot" Pittman | Finished 8th | Sapulpa, OK |
| John Spadavecchia | $219,000 | Miami, FL |
| Robert Turner | $107,000 | Downey, CA |
| Hugh Vincent | $1,482,000 | Palm Gardens, FL |

——————— The Last Hand ———————

**Hamilton's Cards**    **Vincent's Cards**

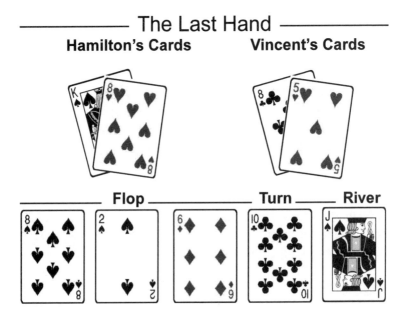

——— Flop ——————— Turn ——— River

| The Finish | Prize Money |
|---|---|
| 1st Hamilton | $ 1,000,000 |
| 2nd Vincent | $ 588,000 |
| 3rd Spadavecchia | $ 294,000 |
| 4th Burgio | $ 168,000 |
| 5th Krux | $ 100,000 |
| 6th Turner | $ 50,400 |
| 7th Aglialoro | $ 43,680 |
| 8th Pittman | $ 38,640 |
| 9th Lott | $ 33,600 |

## How It Happened
### by Tom McEvoy

The final hand of the 1994 WSOP came when Hugh Vincent limped in on the button with the 8♣5♥. Russ Hamilton held the K♠8♥. The flop came 8♠2♠6♦, giving both men top pair. Hamilton checked. Vincent bet $100,000 and Hamilton responded by moving all his chips to the center, raising around $750,000 more. Hamilton had the chip lead so he wasn't going to get broke to the hand, but Vincent would get broke if he called and lost.

What could Hamilton have? His most likely hand was top pair with a better kicker or even an overpair that he had slowplayed. In fact Hamilton had slowplayed a set of queens against Vincent just prior to this hand, trapping him for a lot of chips and doubling through him. This looked like a similar scenario.

Vincent didn't think about it for very long. Chewing on a hamburger, he turned over his hand and said, "I call." This was not a good spot to call because he had no kicker for his eight. He needed to catch a five to win the hand with two pair. The last two cards helped neither opponent and Vincent was eliminated from the tournament, albeit over a half million dollars richer.

Russ Hamilton not only won the championship and $1 million, he was awarded his weight in silver to commemorate the silver anniversary of the World Series of Poker. In a formal ceremony following his victory, tournament officials weighed Hamilton and presented him with 330 pounds of silver bars. At $5.40 per ounce, the silver was worth an additional $28,512 to the champion.

## Highlights

Russ Hamilton made a straight flush in a hand that he played against Vince Burgio, the first-ever straight flush at the final table of the WSOP. The hand doubled up his chips and put him in position to be a contender the rest of the way. There were 3,800 total entries in all the events with $9,969,500 in prize money.

There was no inductee into the Poker Hall of Fame in 1994. The traditional induction had taken place during the Hall of Fame Classic since that tournament's inception in 1988 but because the tournament was not held in 1994, no one was inducted.

# Russ Hamilton
## He's Worth his Weight in Silver
### Interview with a Champ (1996) by Dana Smith

R uss Hamilton is worth not only his weight in gold but his weight in silver as well. He won the $1 million World Series of Poker title during the Horseshoe's silver anniversary celebration in 1994 and as a bonus, the hefty Hamilton was awarded his weight in silver. (I wonder if Jack Binion was secretly hoping that a skinny lightweight would win?)

The champ and his wife Carolyn moved from Detroit to Las Vegas in 1984, about a month after Hamilton, playing golf in the sunshine at the Sahara Country Club, saw a television report of the ice-encrusted roof caving in on the Silverdome in Pontiac. "I looked at the 12 inches of snow on the ground and the cars that had slid off the icy roads," he reflected. "The next day, I bought a house in Vegas, called Carolyn (who was vice-president of a bank) in Detroit to tell her the news, and we moved. It was that simple."

Hamilton was, characteristically, sitting backward in his chair at the $75-$150 H.O.S.E. game at the Mirage when I arrived to interview him. I wondered how he had handled the sudden wealth, glaring spotlight of fame, and other pressures that sometimes accompany victory. Had he run through the money as fast as a lawnmower goes through grass like many of the California lottery winners that I have read about? Had he been offered bizarre business deals, or been hit on by predatory borrowers for a stake? And how had the championship title affected his poker life? The friendly and relaxed champ with the great sense of humor discussed what's changed and what hasn't since winning the tournament.

*You're a fairly recognizable figure. Do people treat you differently now?*

Yes, they do. And it's true that I'm pretty hard to miss! Although I've always had a lot of friends in Las Vegas, people that I don't really know all that well, including total strangers, still come over to congratulate me, even after two years. And all the floor people are extra nice.

*How have you handled the $1 million and silver "change" that you won? Did you take a lavish cruise, buy a Mercedes?*

Before I won the championship, I owned and then sold a burglar alarm business in Las Vegas that was very successful. I also had done well in poker and with my basketball betting. So the money really hasn't changed my lifestyle all that much. I still drive the same car, but I did buy a nicer house. And no, I haven't taken a vacation in years. But I do gamble higher on the golf course. Come to think of it, my golf is something that *has* changed since 1994. After I won the WSOP, every golf hustler in the country came running, thinking that they were going to win some of that money. They came and they went. They weren't very successful at what they tried to do.

*You wager in poker, golf and basketball—anything else?*

I still play a little blackjack, and I used to play tournaments other than poker (blackjack, dice, and baccarat) along with my wife, who still plays a few of them.

*Are you primarily a tournament poker player or do you prefer playing ring games?*

I'm mostly a ring-game player. I enter very few tournaments, primarily pot-limit Omaha or no-limit hold'em events, and I don't travel for them. I just play the WSOP, Queens and Hall of Fame.

*Why do you prefer playing pot-limit and no-limit poker?*

Because they're much better games and require far more skill. In no-limit hold'em, you can trap people, you can finesse them, you can outplay them. If you commit an error in limit poker, you've still got chips left to play; but if you make one mistake in no-limit poker, you're history. We used to have a pot-limit Omaha game going all the time at the Shoe—small games with $5-$10 blinds and bigger games up to $50-$100 blinds, depending on who was in town. Then about eight months before the '94 *WSOP,* we lost that game and began playing Omaha/8 instead. Still, around tournament time, pot-limit Omaha is very popular in the side action.

*In your opinion, what are some of the bad habits of professional poker players?*

This is the weirdest profession in the world. Up until a few years ago, most of the WSOP champions went broke after they won the tournament. Of course, that's not unusual among gamblers. A lot of them have bad habits, either in the pits or in sports betting (very few of them with drugs). Not very many of them go broke playing poker.

*What's alluring about sports betting?*

It's the thrill of watching the game, sweating it, having money on it. It's action. It amazes me that, as smart as some professional poker players are, they go out and blow it in the pits on dice or baccarat, knowing that they don't have an edge. In sports, you can get an edge if you know what you're doing, but most of them just want to gamble. And that's what they do—and why they go broke.

*Have you been hit up often for money for loans or business deals since '94?*

Oh, yes! They came out of the woodwork. Everybody's got a business that they want to go into, or they need a stake for a poker game or a tournament. There's just no end to it.

*Do you stake tournament players?*

Not very often. I've done it with just a few guys, winning players only, who've run into hard times. I'm close to even, but I don't consider backing tournament players to be a good investment; it's too risky. It's a much better deal for the players. I wasn't backed for the '94 series. I always put up my own money.

*What's the biggest mistake that tournament players make?*

Most of them don't want to play only their best games; they want to play every game; they want to be in constant action.

*So if winning the WSOP didn't change your lifestyle all that much, what has it meant to you?*

Winning the championship was something that I wanted more than anything else in the world because it puts you into an elite group of poker players that very few people can enter. When we got down to six players, the money never ever was in question. When we got down to three players and then two players, it was never the money. There was only one thing that mattered— having my picture on the wall and winning the bracelet.

Prior to the championship event, I played a pot-limit Omaha tournament. When we got down to five-handed action, they wanted to make a deal (I had the majority of the chips at the time). So we made a deal in which I got $100,000, the next guy about $90,000, and so on. When we resumed play, I told them, "Guys, I'm putting my money in the first pot and whoever wants the bracelet, just come and play with me because I'm going home." Within two hands, I was gone. Winning that pot-limit Omaha bracelet didn't mean anything to me. I had done what I had come to accomplish, I had won the money. But when it came to the title event, you couldn't have forced me to accept even $200,000 extra to let someone else have a chance at winning it. I didn't want the money: I wanted the championship.

*Who came in second in '94?*

Some guy from Florida (laughing). Does anybody ever remember who came in second?

"Chips don't have a home. If money is your God, you can forget no-limit poker, because it's going to hurt you too much to turn loose of it. The way I feel about those pieces of green paper is that you can't take them with you, and they may not have much value in five years time, but right now I can take them and trade them in for pleasure, or bring pleasure to other people. If they wanted you to hold onto money, they'd have made it with handles on it."

— Jack Straus

"It's important to take time to prepare yourself. If you don't feel good and don't have a positive attitude, it seems like you're less likely to have a rewarding experience." — Brad Daugherty

"They can take the money, they can take the silver, but they can never take that picture off the wall."

— Russ Hamilton upon winning the championship in 1994

# 1995 World Championship Event
## 26th World Series of Poker
### Number of Entries: 273

## ———— The Championship Table ————

| The Finalists | Chip Count | Hometown |
|---|---|---|
| Dolph Arnold | Finished 9th | Houston, TX |
| Brent Carter | $319,000 | Oak Park, IL |
| Hamid Dastmalchi | $232,000 | San Diego, CA |
| Barbara Enright | $199,000 | Van Nuys, CA |
| Tom Franklin | Finished 7th | Gulfport, MS |
| Howard Goldfarb | $1,194,000 | Toronto, Canada |
| Dan Harrington | $532,000 | Downey, CA |
| Henry Orenstein | Finished 8th | Verona, NJ |
| Chuck Thompson | $254,000 | Santa Cruz, CA |

## —————— The Last Hand ——————

### Harrington's Cards          Goldfarb's Cards

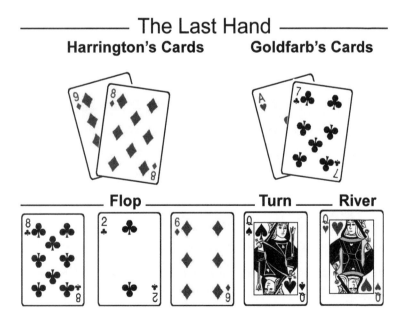

Flop ———————— Turn ——— River

136

| The Finish | Prize Money |
|------------|-------------|
| 1st Harrington | $ 1,000,000 |
| 2nd Goldfarb | $ 519,000 |
| 3rd Carter | $ 302,000 |
| 4th Dastmalchi | $ 173,000 |
| 5th Enright | $ 114,180 |
| 6th Thompson | $ 86,500 |
| 7th Franklin | $ 69,200 |
| 8th Orenstein | $ 51,900 |
| 9th Arnold | $ 39,790 |

## How It Happened

Dan Harrington, an attorney and professional poker player, led Canadian poker player Howard Goldfarb $1,697,000 to $1,033,000 in chips when they began playing heads-up. With an ante of $3,000 and the blinds at $15,000-$30,000, the final hand came down when Goldfarb raised $100,000 before the flop with A-7 offsuit and Harrington called with 9-8 suited. On the flop Harrington checked and Goldfarb went all in for $617,000. Barely hesitating, Harrington called with top pair. The two queens that fell on fourth and fifth streets helped neither player, and Dan Harrington became the 1995 World Champion of Poker.

Earlier during the Series, Harrington won the $2,500 buy-in no-limit hold'em tournament after winning a one-table satellite. He then won his seat in the championship event via a supersatellite. Better known as a chess player, Harrington entered only two tournaments and won them both to make his batting average perfect. His WSOP winnings through 2002 totaled $1,325,858.

## Highlights

For the first time in WSOP history, a woman finished among the top six players at the final table of the championship event. To date no woman has finished higher than Barbara Enright, who came in fifth.

At the players' request, Chinese poker was added to the WSOP tournament schedule. It was to become the shortest-lived event in WSOP history when it was removed from the events list after 1996. No one was inducted into the Poker Hall of Fame.

# Barbara Enright
## The First Lady at the Last Table
### Interview with a Champ (1997) by Dana Smith

Barbara Enright, a two-time Ladies World Champion, has finished higher than any other woman in the World Series of Poker championship event, placing fifth in 1995. She followed that accomplishment by winning the WSOP pot-limit hold'em tournament in 1996, and had just won the $500 buy-in limit hold'em event at the Queens Classic when I tracked her down at the Commerce Casino in Los Angeles. The conversation was brisk as Enright, Max Shapiro (her significant other), Linda Johnson, Mike Sexton and I talked about poker, love, fame and fortune.

The energetic maven of tournament poker, Enright recently was featured in a high-profile *Elle* magazine article titled "Luck Be a Lady," in which the magazine called her "the most celebrated female tournament player." The subtitle played on a topic that is growing more and more ho-hum in poker circles: "Taking advantage of male insecurity is just one way women are beating the pants off men in the macho world of high-stakes poker." But Enright takes that cliche in stride: "Ninety-eight percent of poker players treat me like everyone else. They know me and respect me."

"Most women who play poker are very nice people," Johnson added. "But the Elle article portrayed them as being cold and calculating. I was very disappointed in it, because I don't think that's the way most female poker players are."

Shapiro observed that "When a general magazine writes an article about poker players, it needs an angle. *Elle* stereotyped all the women as being domineering or using their femininity to overcome the men." Certainly, the slick did not picture "the softer side of Sears," to use another cliche, in its interviews with star female poker players Enright, Annie Duke, Jennifer Harman, Cissy Bottoms and Cyndy Violette. A source of far greater stress than the gender bias hypothecated by the magazine article is the personal pressure that Enright must handle when she is routinely described as the world's greatest female poker player. She is surprisingly modest in her reaction to that unsolicited title: "I am honored, of course, but it is a dubious title. There are many great women players who don't enter tournaments—the women who play in the higher-limit cash games are great players."

*Elle* featured a photo of Enright stepping out of "her" Rolls Royce. Shapiro explained that, "When the editor asked Barbara what kind of car she drove, being a smart aleck, she said, 'Oh, I drive a Rolls Royce.' Then I get this panic call from her and she says, 'Max, they're sending a hair dresser and a make-up artist and a photographer to photograph me in my Rolls. What do I do now?' I told her that she'd better find a Rolls real quick. Luckily, she got Len Miller to loan her his."

The colorful, competitive (and very witty) Enright is highly sought after these days for interviews—her schedule is longer than *Gone With the Wind*. She has been featured in the *Chicago Tribune, Las Vegas Sun*, and TV's *Inside Edition*. But this time around, we declared "time out" and decided to just talk "fun" stuff.

*What attracted you to poker as a profession?*

Freedom! The freedom to stay in bed when I don't feel well and to take a vacation when I want to. I like not being regimented to a time schedule. My mom once told me that I should get a job delivering Chinese food so that I would never go broke, but I haven't had to resort to that yet. I enjoy playing tournaments, the travel, meeting new people.

*Is it true that you have a few pet peeves in poker?*

Yes. For example, when you're playing a tournament and you go all-in, why do people always say, "Good luck!" You don't want anybody left in it except you, so why lie about it? Then somebody will bust you and say, "I'm sorry." If she were that sorry, why would she bust you?! And why do dealers say "possible straight" in seven-card stud? Why don't they also say "two pair, possible full house?" There is supposed to be only one player to a hand, so why should dealers help out by reading the cards for players?

*Do you feel pressure because*

*of your high finish at the WSOP?*

Sometimes, yes. No one is infallible and anything can happen in poker, you know.

*Do you get a kick out of being selected as a bounty in events such as Bay 101's "Shooting Star" tournament?*

I get a free buy-in ($1,000), and that's a kick. But I also played the $8 buy-in ladies tournament at the Bicycle Club and came in fourth. I took a bad beat: I had A-10 and my opponent had A-4. An ace came on the flop and I had her beaten until she caught a four on the river to bust me out of the tournament.

*You sound as disappointed over not winning that one as you would be if you lost a big event. How so?*

It's the competition—and it's just like letting $1,600 slip through my fingers.

*You have the reputation of being a rather aggressive player. How does one learn to be aggressive in poker?*

I don't think it's something that you can learn. You're either aggressive or you're not. I am a very aggressive person in life; I try to push everyone around. (Shapiro, Barbara's significant other, pointed to himself at this comment.) Yeah, Max really looks pushed around, doesn't he?!

*Linda Johnson:* Barbara won her first WSOP ladies championship in 1986 and I came in third. I would compare playing against Barbara to being run over by a Mack truck. She never lets up. Barbara doesn't know how to limp in—how would you describe her attitude toward limping, Max?

*Max Shapiro:* "Shoot 'em up, Buttercup!" She doesn't know the meaning of the word!

*Enright:* Limp is a five-letter word spelled r-a-i-s-e! But I only raise with "quality" hands. Like today in the $8 tournament, I raised with the 6♣ 3♣ on the button. The flop came with a three and a deuce-something, with two clubs. On the turn came another three and on the river came the third club. That hand left them talking to themselves.

*Somebody told me that toward the end of a tournament, you are a card rack. True?*

Me, a card rack? Today at the end of the ladies tournament, I had the worst beats in the world, one after the other—not just bad beats, killer beats. So that's not true. I played a few hands very well and the lady sitting next to me said, "You sure are lucky." Sure, I hit a couple of flops, but if I hadn't hit them, I would have released the hand—I know how to do that.

*Does a player make his own luck?*

Absolutely! All the great tournament players put themselves in a position to get lucky, and so they get lucky more often than others. But I'm not a lucky player—if I were lucky, I would have won the World Series in 1995.

*You were the first woman to make the final table at the Big One. What was that like—a lot of hype, pressure, support?*

The fans were incredible. I couldn't believe that there were so many people rooting for somebody they didn't know. A man called the tournament secretary and asked, "Is the lady still in it? I don't know her, but I'm rooting for her."

*Max Shapiro:* On one hand that she bet, a couple of players said, "I don't want to call her because I don't want to get booed out of here."

*But Brent Carter didn't seem to mind calling you. How did your final hand come down, Barbara?*

Everybody had passed and I was in the big blind with two eights. Brent was in the small blind with a 6-3 and he completed the blind. Then I moved all-in and he called me. Brent flopped two pair to knock me out of the tournament.

*Was his call correct?*

I don't think so. If he was willing to match my chips, he should have moved in with the 6-3 in the first place to try to get me off the hand, to rob me—that would have been a good play. But he just limped. He didn't know that I would raise. I could have been sitting there with a 9-2 and beaten him on the flop by catching a pair of nines. With a 6-3, what could he expect to beat? Brent told me later that he thought I was bluffing him when I moved in all of my chips.

*Do you think that, because of your aggressive reputation, people sometimes call you with lesser hands because they think you're bluffing?*

Yes. And I like that because when I get hands, I'm always going to get paid off. Of course, sometimes it's a disadvantage because they will chase me down. And that's what happened at the final table in 1995. Incidentally, I won my seat for that tournament in a supersatellite. Just before I played it, I asked a player named "Porkchop" if he wanted to stake me for the $220 buy-in. He said no, because he was leaving town. That cost him $57,000.

*When you win big-big money in a tournament, do you invest it or what?*

I don't like to discuss my finances, but I can tell you one thing: I live good! I try to get full value out of life.

*Other poker professionals have told me that maintaining a good personal relationship is tough.*

That's probably because a lot of people don't understand this business. But if you're with somebody who understands it or who also is in the poker world, I don't think that it's difficult. They know what you're doing when you leave them. I met Max at the Legends of Poker tournament at the Bicycle Club, where we were both "legends." I never play Omaha high-low, but I played in that event because Max was the host. I didn't win his bounty, but I think I lasted longer than he did.

*How do you handle Barbara's fame, Max?*

*Max Shapiro:* (laughing) Being such a poker celebrity myself, it is difficult being eclipsed by her fame, but I bask in her glory. Seriously, in addition to being such a tough poker player, she is quite a lady. That's what makes her so remarkable.

*Have you ever been a passive player, Barbara?*

Not since I was four years old when I was playing with my older brother for matchsticks. When we began playing for pennies, I ran over him.

*Mike Sexton:* Barbara is the most dominating, relentless, aggressive woman on the tournament circuit. She strikes fear in all the top male players; when she's at the table, their hearts are pounding. I don't care what they say, that's the truth of the matter.

Tom McEvoy, 1983 champion, with $540,000 in prize money. His WSOP winnings as of 2002 were $1,207,622. In the background (l to r) are Teddy Binion, Jack Binion and Bobby Baldwin.

Berry Johnston, 1986 WSOP Champion, surveying $570,000 in prize money. Through 2002 he had won $1,888,527.

1994 WSOP champion Russ Hamilton (l) at the championship table with John Spadavecchia (third place) and Hugh Vincent (runner-up). Through 2002 Hamilton's WSOP winnings totaled $1,101,065.

# 1996 World Championship Event
## 27th World Series of Poker
### Number of Entries: 295

—————— The Championship Table ——————

| The Finalists | Chip Count | Hometown |
| --- | --- | --- |
| Steve Beam | Finished 9th | Las Vegas, NV |
| John Bonetti | $794,000 | Houston, TX |
| Andre Boyer | $153,000 | Las Vegas, NV |
| Fernando Fisdel | Finished 8th | New York, NY |
| Men Nguyen | $252,000 | Bell Gardens, CA |
| J.P. Schmalz | Finished 7th | Unknown |
| Huck Seed | $632,000 | Las Vegas, NV |
| An Tran | $596,000 | Las Vegas, NV |
| Bruce Van Horn | $524,000 | Ada, OK |

—————— The Last Hand ——————

**Seed's Cards**     **Van Horn's Cards**

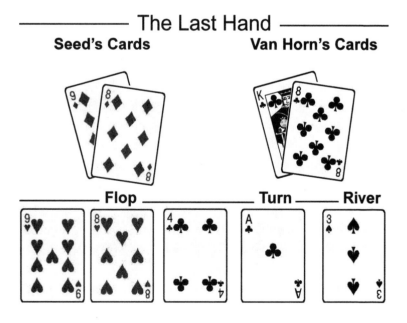

—————— Flop —————— Turn —————— River

144

| The Finish | Prize Money |
|------------|-------------|
| 1st  Seed | $ 1,000,000 |
| 2nd Van Horn | $  585,000 |
| 3rd Bonetti | $  341,250 |
| 4th Nguyen | $  195,000 |
| 5th Tran | $  128,700 |
| 6th Boyer | $   97,500 |
| 7th Schmalz | $   78,000 |
| 8th Fisdel | $   58,500 |
| 9th Beam | $   44,850 |

## How It Happened

When Huck Seed and Dr. Bruce Van Horn began playing heads-up, Van Horn had a 2-to-1 chip advantage. In a key hand prior to their final confrontation, Van Horn raised before the flop with A-J, Seed reraised all in with pocket queens, and Van Horn called. Seed doubled his stack and took the chip lead when his queens held up.

In the final hand, Van Horn raised before the flop with K-8 suited and Seed called with 9-8 suited. On the flop, Seed bet his two pair, Van Horn raised, and Seed reraised. Van Horn called the raise all in. When a suited ace came on the turn, Van Horn had a flush draw but when no help came on the river, Seed won the $2,328,000 pot. The 1996 championship, $1 million and the gold bracelet were awarded to the 28-year-old professional poker player. After experiencing the thrill of near-victory by defeating 293 players in the biggest game in town, Dr. Van Horn, an amateur player from Ada, Oklahoma, returned home a half-million dollars richer to continue supporting the community activities for which he is highly respected in his hometown.

## Highlights

Julius Oral "Little Man" Popwell, a famous road gambler who played with Johnny Moss in the '40s and '50s, was posthumously inducted into the Poker Hall of Fame.

# 1997 World Championship Event
## 28th World Series of Poker
### Number of Entries: 312

##### ———— The Championship Table ————

| The Finalists | Chip Count | Hometown |
|---|---|---|
| Peter Bao | $204,000 | Las Vegas, NV |
| Chris Bjorin | Finished 9th | London, England |
| Mel Judah | $301,000 | London, England |
| David Roepke | Finished 8th | Unknown |
| Tormod Roren | Finished 7th | Unknown |
| Ron Stanley | $694,000 | Las Vegas, NV |
| John Strzemp | $245,000 | Las Vegas, NV |
| Stu Ungar | $1,066,000 | Las Vegas, NV |
| Bob Walker | $611,000 | Las Vegas, NV |

##### ———— The Last Hand ————

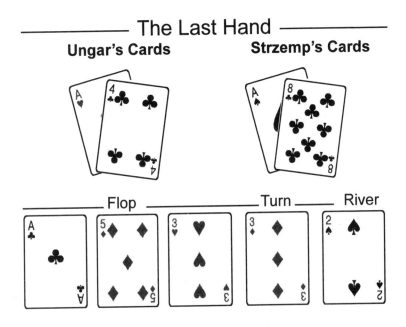

**Ungar's Cards**  **Strzemp's Cards**

——— Flop ——— Turn —— River

| The Finish | Prize Money |
| --- | --- |
| 1st Ungar | $ 1,000,000 |
| 2nd Strzemp | $ 583,000 |
| 3rd Judah | $ 371,000 |
| 4th Stanley | $ 212,000 |
| 5th Walker | $ 161,120 |
| 6th Bao | $ 127,200 |
| 7th Roren | $ 95,400 |
| 8th Roepke | $ 63,600 |
| 9th Bjorin | $ 48,760 |

## How It Happened
### by Tom McEvoy

By the time Stu Ungar and John Strzemp got heads up, Strzemp was at a 3-to-1 chip disadvantage. The end came after only six hands. Ungar raised to $40,000 before the flop and Strzemp called. Ungar held an A-4 offsuit and Strzemp held an A-8 offsuit, putting Strzemp out front with the better kicker. The A-5-3 flop maintained Strzemp's lead, but it also gave Ungar a gutshot straight draw. Strzemp bet $120,000 on the flop, Ungar moved in on him, and Strzemp called. On fourth street came another three, pairing the board and keeping Strzemp's hand in the lead. Ungar won his third championship title when the 2♠ fell on the river to complete the straight.

This dramatic finish was not the first time that Ungar had won the title by making a gutshot wheel on the final hand. In 1980 the brash, young rookie got heads up with the legendary Doyle Brunson and hit a wheel card on fourth street to break Brunson.

Strzemp earlier had won three key hands that moved him up the chip ladder. Against third-place finisher Mel Judah, who had raised with an A-J, Strzemp defended his blind with the 9♣ 7♣. Strzemp flopped a flush draw with a gutshot straight draw against Judah's top two pair, doubling up when he made the flush. Against Ron Stanley, who started the final table in second-chip position, Strzemp got all his chips in before the flop with pocket tens against Stanley's pocket kings. When a winning 10 appeared on fourth street, Strzemp took over the second-chip lead. Apparently unnerved by this turn of events, Stanley later made a play at the pot with a J-8 only to get eliminated in fourth place by Strzemp's pocket aces.

## Highlights

The final table of six contestants was played on a stage in the middle of The Fremont Street Experience. Spectators sat in bleachers to watch the action under the hot afternoon sun.

1997 was the first year that a husband and wife both won gold bracelets. Maria Stern won for seven-card stud and Max Stern won two events, seven-card stud high-low split and no-limit hold'em. Linda Johnson won the seven-card razz event, making two women who won bracelets in open events that year. 1997 also was the first year that the World Series of Poker main event drew over 300 entries. And it was the last year that the Horseshoe published an elaborate brochure-magazine.

Stu Ungar joined Johnny Moss as the only two players in WSOP history to win the championship event three times. Roger Moore was inducted into the Poker Hall of Fame.

## John Strzemp
### A 1997 Conversation with Dana Smith

As the agile acrobats were preparing for the evening's performance of Mystere and the pirates were winning one more fiery battle in front of Treasure Island, the man who oversees all their efforts, and those of the 4,500 other employees of the hotel casino, was preparing to do battle against five of the best poker players in the world. Although he wasn't quite as successful as his perennially victorious pirates, Treasure Island president John Strzemp made a valiant effort to protect his ship against the final-table marauders at the World Series of Poker. Coming in second to the legendary Stu Ungar ain't all that bad, especially for a recreational player.

Watching the final table play from the bleachers in the middle of the Fremont Street Experience, it seemed to me that Strzemp had opened up his game. Was that part of his game plan? "I didn't have a detailed game plan," Strzemp said, "but I knew that some very tough players were at the table and that they probably would play very aggressive poker. You only get so many opportunities to be there, so I definitely didn't want to play passively and allow myself to get run over. I had played with Stu Ungar at a couple of tables during the event and I knew what a terrific player he is."

Obviously Strzemp did not get run over. He did get lucky,

particularly in an all-in pot he played against Stanley, who was holding pocket kings to Strzemp's pocket tens. "I had all my chips in on that one. Judah announced that he had mucked a 10 and so when the flop came with no 10, I was preparing to leave. I got fortunate when a 10 came on the turn to win the hand for me. At that point I thought, 'Hey, maybe this is my day after all.'

"You have to capitalize on luck when it comes. We all have days when we play really well and times when our luck is running good. When those two dovetail, that's what I call 'situational' luck, getting lucky at the right times. You hear players say, 'I haven't had pocket aces in nine years!' But it's not so much a matter of how frequently you get aces, it's *when* you get them, what they're matched up against, and how you handle them that counts."

Strzemp handled aces perfectly in a deceptive move that knocked Stanley out in fourth place. "I was in the big blind with pocket aces and Ron put in a raise before the flop. I just called because it was consistent with other times when I had called with a relatively loose hand. It could have backfired if the flop had come out wrong, but I thought it was the perfect situation in which to smooth-call. And it worked out okay for me."

Was there a special benefit—in addition to the half-million dollars he won, of course—that Strzemp gained from playing at the final table of the World Series of Poker? "One of the ironies of poker is that you can improve your own game simply by playing with people who are better than you are. The people that you compete with over the years become your teachers. And Stu Ungar is unbelievably fantastic. He played extremely aggressively, very confidently—he's tough!"

"That was by far my greatest performance ever. It was so tough to come back."
— Stu Ungar to Jack Binion at the 1997 WSOP

"Four days ago nobody wanted to speak to me. Looks like things might be a little different now."
— Stu Ungar to reporters after winning in 1997

## Stu Ungar (1953-1998)
### "The Comeback Kid Has Cashed Out"
by Dana Smith

It was a scorcher as I squeezed into the bleachers surrounding the raised platform in the middle of Fremont Street where the 1997 World Series of Poker finale was being played. But the blistering temperature seemed to go unnoticed by the six men sitting at the championship table, perhaps because they were enveloped by the far more intense heat of battle. One of them would walk away with the spoils of victory—$1 million and the prize they coveted even more than the money, the gold bracelet that forever identifies the victor as a member of an exclusive club that admits only one new member per year. Only one player at the championship table already was a member of the club—Stu "The Kid" Ungar—and he was the drawing card. Nobody had heard much about "Stuey" during his decade-long hiatus from poker, but still it was a foregone conclusion that he was going to win.

Putting on the heat is an understatement of how Ungar used his uncanny reading ability, poker skills and huge pile of chips to club his opponents into submission. Wielding perfectly timed weapons such as slowplay and the bluff, he marched confidently forward to the kill. Carving his name even deeper into the stone tablets of WSOP history, he made an unparalled comeback from near obscurity to win his third World Championship of Poker.

It was the first time I had seen Ungar play—and the last time that most of us would ever see him alive. In November, 1998, "The Comeback Kid" died at the age of 45, the victim of his vices. Like the flawed hero in a Shakespearean tragedy, Ungar's genius at cards was undermined by his vulnerability to self-destructive habits. "I did coke to keep up," he disclosed to *Icon* magazine several months after his victory. "You use it as an excuse to stay up and play poker. But then you take it home with you. When you have access to it and the money don't mean nothing—it's a sickness. I guarantee you it's taken 10, 15 years off my life."

Ungar began his life in New York in 1953, the son of a bookmaker. At the age of 10 he learned to play gin rummy, the first card game to bring him fame and fortune. Four years later, after the death of both his father and mother, Ungar dropped out of school. He began playing and defeating the best gin rummy players in New York, but often squandered his winnings at the racetrack. Later, he satiated his taste for high-stakes gambling by betting sports.

"Ungar's gambling losses in New York sent him fleeing to Las Vegas in the late 1970s, one step ahead of a bookmaker to whom he owed a five-figure debt," Ed Koch reported in the *Las Vegas Sun*. "He scraped together $1,500 and entered a Las Vegas gin rummy tournament. He won the $50,000 first prize to pay off his bookie debt." It wasn't long before he could no longer find anybody to play gin rummy against him, so Ungar turned to the second card game for which he became famous, blackjack. That, too, was short-lived—he was banned from blackjack tables in every Las Vegas casino because of his infallible card-counting skills.

In fact he accepted a wager from Bob Stupak, then owner of Vegas World and future designer of Stratosphere Tower, to count down the last three decks in a six-deck shoe of cards, 156 cards. Stupak would pay Ungar $100,000 if he could do it perfectly; Ungar would pay $10,000 if he failed. He didn't miss a single call.

Stupak remained a supportive friend to "The Kid," and just before Ungar died in '98 he signed a contract to back him in a second comeback attempt at poker, the third card game that had brought Ungar riches. "I felt he was a good investment," Stupak told Koch. Ungar could have become a stellar investment indeed. "He won 10 major no-limit hold'em championship events with $5,000 or higher buy-ins," Mike Sexton reported in *Card Player*. "And he was the only man in history to capture titles at both the WSOP and the ($10,000 buy-in) Super Bowl of Poker."

But it was his skill at gin rummy that Ungar was the proudest. "Someday, I suppose it's possible for someone to be a better no-limit hold'em player than me. I doubt it, but it could happen," he told Sexton in 1997. "But I swear to you, I don't see how anyone could ever play gin better than me." Few would doubt that he was right, but many would question his ability to win at the much higher-stakes game of life. As John L. Smith said in the *Las Vegas Review-Journal*, "Cards were never 'The Kid's' problem."

# 1998 World Championship Event
## 29th World Series of Poker
### Number of Entries: 350

## ———— The Championship Table ————

| The Finalists | Chip Count | Hometown |
|---|---|---|
| Mark Brochard | Finished 8th | France |
| T.J. Cloutier | $829,000 | Richardson, TX |
| Jan Lundberg | Finished 7th | London, England |
| Kevin McBride | $873,000 | Boca Raton, FL |
| Paul McKinney | Finished 9th | Princeton, WV |
| Scotty Nguyen | $1,184,000 | Henderson, NV |
| Ben Roberts | Finished 6th | London, England |
| Lee Salem | $240,000 | San Diego, CA |
| Dewey Weum | $376,000 | Monona, WI |

## ———— The Last Hand ————

**Nguyen's Cards**  **McBride's Cards**

Flop ———————— Turn ——— River

| The Finish | Prize Money |
|---|---|
| 1st Nguyen | $1,000,000 |
| 2nd McBride | $ 687,500 |
| 3rd Cloutier | $ 437,500 |
| 4th Weum | $ 250,000 |
| 5th Salem | $ 190,000 |
| 6th Roberts | $ 150,000 |
| 7th Lundberg | $ 112,500 |
| 8th Brochard | $ 75,000 |
| 9th McKinney | $ 57,500 |

## How It Happened

Before the flop, 40-year-old investments consultant Kevin McBride raised $50,000 holding a Q-10. With the inferior hand but superior chip position, 35-year-old Scotty Nguyen, a former Vietnamese refugee and professional poker player, called with J-9 offsuit. When the flop came with two nines, Nguyen checked. With an inside straight draw and two overcards, McBride bet $100,000. Nguyen thought for a while before calling. The turn card brought another eight, improving Nguyen's hand from trip nines to a full house. He again checked in a deceptive move designed to trap McBride, who bet another $100,000 with his straight-flush draw. Nguyen flat-called the bet. When the 8♠ fell on the river, Nguyen bet $310,000, enough to put McBride all in if he called. While McBride was pondering what to do, Nguyen stated, "You call, gonna be all over, baby." After further deliberation, McBride answered, "I call. I play the board." Nguyen then turned up his winning nine verifying that indeed it was all over. His total winnings at the WSOP through 2002 were $1,697,272.

## Highlights

For the first time in WSOP history, only five players appeared at the televised championship table. The night before the final table began, with seven players left in action, Scotty Nguyen knocked out two of them at one time with a winning flush. Because of the cancellation of the Hall of Fame Classic, no one was inducted into the Poker Hall of Fame during the years 1998-2000.

# 1999 World Championship Event
## 30th World Series of Poker
### Number of Entries: 393

———— The Championship Table ————

| The Finalists | Chip Count | Hometown |
|---|---|---|
| Stanley "Ty" Bayne | Finished 9th | Visalia, CA |
| Chris Bigler | $319,000 | Fislisbad, Switzerland |
| Noel Furlong | $1,544,000 | Clifton Lodge, Ireland |
| Alan Goehring | $828,000 | New York, NY |
| George McKeever | Finished 7th | Dublin, Ireland |
| Padraig Parkinson | $674,000 | Dublin, Ireland |
| Paul Rowe | Finished 8th | Las Vegas, NV |
| Huck Seed | $402,000 | Las Vegas, NV |
| Erik Seidel | $167,000 | Henderson, NV |

———— The Last Hand ————

**Furlong's Cards**      **Goehring's Cards**

———— Flop ————      — Turn —      — River —

| The Finish | Prize Money |
|---|---|
| 1st Furlong | $1,000,000 |
| 2nd Goehring | $ 768,625 |
| 3rd Parkinson | $ 489,125 |
| 4th Seidel | $ 279,500 |
| 5th Bigler | $ 212,420 |
| 6th Seed | $ 167,700 |
| 7th McKeever | $ 125,775 |
| 8th Rowe | $ 83,850 |
| 9th Bayne | $ 64,285 |

## How It Happened

Irish carpet manufacturer Noel Furlong limped into the pot from the button before the flop and New Yorker Alan Goehring flat-called. On the flop both players checked. On the turn card, Goehring checked and Furlong bet $150,000. Goehring raised $300,000 and, after a short deliberation, Furlong moved all his chips into the middle putting Goehring to the test. If 36-year-old Goehring folds, he will be at a $3.5 million to $400,000 chip disadvantage to Furlong. If he calls and doesn't win the pot, he will become the runner-up for the championship. Goehring called the raise by pushing the rest of his chips into the pot and with no help on the river, came in second to Furlong, albeit three-quarters of $1 million richer.

At age 61 Furlong became only the second non-professional poker player to win the World Series title and the ninth champion to win $1 million for his efforts. "Because of Noel's victory, I think that a lot of people now look at the World Series in a different way," Erik Seidel commented. "If he can do it, why can't I?" Through 2002 Furlong had won $1,070,785 at the WSOP.

## Highlights

Furlong won his seat via a satellite, as do the majority of players in the modern era of the WSOP. The Series featured 16 preliminary events, attracted 3,456 players, and paid out $11,291,000 in prize money. The purse at the WSOP continues to dwarf the purse at Wimbledon, the Masters, the Kentucky Derby and baseball's World Series. 1999 was the first year that the WSOP was held without Jack Binion at the helm.

# Noel Furlong
## The Champ Pays Tribute to a Pioneer & Dear Friend
### Interview with a Champ (2001) by Dana Smith

There's something charming about an Irish brogue and in the case of Noel Furlong, it doesn't stop with the accent. Admittedly shy by nature and somewhat reclusive by choice, the gracious Irish gentleman held informal counsel to a perpetual line of poker players, friends, and well-wishers just outside the entrance to the bingo-hall-turned-tournament-room at the Horseshoe Casino during the 2001 World Series of Poker. As we began our interview to the cacophony of poker chips click-clacking in the background, Padraig Parkinson, third-place finisher to Furlong at the '99 WSOP, stopped by to say hello to his friend and fellow countryman, mentioning that he had seen Furlong on TV.

"Would you mind doing this interview for me?" Furlong asked, referring to the fact that he had never before granted an interview because, admittedly, he is a very private person.

"No, I'm not world famous, I'm only the friend of a world-famous player," Parkinson replied with the smile for which the Irish are famous.

Sadly, Furlong's lifelong friend Terry Rogers was not able to greet him at the Series this year. A year after rejoicing in seeing one of his lifetime dreams come true when two Irishmen played the final table in the WSOP $10,000 championship event, Rogers died. We began by talking about the famous Irish bookmaker and pioneer in promoting global poker tournaments who accompanied Furlong on the "Irish Expedition" to the Series in 1999.

"I got started playing poker in 1984 when I wandered into the Killiney Castle Hotel, where Terry Rogers was running a big tournament. I sat down in a cash game and although I didn't know how to play poker very well, I won because I was "batting," just shoving out my money. After that I began playing at the Eccentric Club, which Terry founded to promote the Irish Open tournaments. The first time I played in the Irish Open, I finished second with Terry advising me while I was playing. I then went on to win it three times, finished second twice, and third once in the late '80s and early '90s. I came to Las Vegas the first time with Terry in 1989 and got to the final table of the championship event, purely by luck. There might be a possibility that I know a little more about how to play poker now, but I definitely didn't know a lot about it then. I was money leader at one point and should've done better, but I finished in sixth place."

*Ten years after placing sixth, you claimed the title in 1999. I've heard that you don't really need that million you won, so I wonder if you might make me a small loan? Just joking, Noel.*

I don't think there's anyone who can't use a million dollars. I was delighted to get it and it has come in very useful. We don't pay taxes on gaming in Ireland, you know.

*When I interviewed Terry Rogers in 1996, he told me that he had traveled to the WSOP with you.*

Terry brought me every year that I came. When I say that he "brought me," what I mean is that every year he would ring me six weeks beforehand and I would say, "Yes, I'll go, Terry." And then about a week before the Series, I would decline. In 1999 he rang me four days beforehand and said, "I've two first-class tickets. You have to come." So I had to do it.

*It must have been gratifying for Terry to see three Irishmen finish so high in the money—you, Parkinson and McKeever. I saw Terry in the audience and thought that maybe you fellows had an extra incentive to take the title home to Ireland, a "win one for the Gipper" sort of thing.*

I think that Terry's biggest aim was to see some Irish fellow win it because he had done so much to publicize the World Series, and he did it without asking to get paid for his efforts. He did everything he could to promote the Series, even ran satellites for it in Ireland. In the early days Jack Binion used to announce the Irish Open during the WSOP.

*In fact, Rogers did a lot to promote international competition in poker.*

Yes, and he brought a lot of Irish out here every year, maybe five to ten people in the early years; today you have thirty and forty coming. He created that desire to be here.

*In that sense, Rogers was a true pioneer. Did you and he play poker together often in Ireland?*

No, we gambled together at horse racing but we seldom played poker together. I'm in the carpeting distribution business—a fairly consequential business that takes a lot of running—and so I don't play poker on a regular basis.

*Terry used to be the biggest bookie in Ireland.*

Yes, he was a very big bookie and a colorful one at that. We have a "festival of racing" that runs at the end of July and beginning of August that possibly is our most popular meeting. It is held at Galway Races in the most western city in Ireland. Very early Terry appreciated that part of a successful firm is to get noticed. All of his staff members used to wear big fluffy straw hats that looked something like a sombrero. This was very unusual in Ireland and it attracted a lot of attention.

In Ireland we have live hare coursing where three dogs chase a hare. The eventual winner might run six or eight times in one day as he eliminates the competition. It's sometimes like playing head-to-head in poker. Three big cups are awarded at the premier meeting, which is Clonmell, and Terry was renowned for the odds that he gave for cross, doubles, and trebles. In other words, you had to pick two winners or three winners. I think that he was the only oddsmaker who understood the odds properly. He was totally in a class of his own at this.

*He offered something like a trifecta and daily double?*

Yes, all those things—and before computers were ever heard

of. He was brilliant with numbers, understood betting and the betting industry better than anybody I knew. He was commonly known by his nickname, "The Red Menace," because he had bright red hair as a younger man.

*And you were close friends with The Red Menace?*

Yes, possibly one of his best friends. He and I were born 100 yards apart in Dunlaoghaire County, Dublin. There was always a bit of friendly rivalry between us, we were two small-town boys.

*Now let's talk about you. Was your father in the carpet business, was it a family thing?*

No, my father owned a large snooker hall. It was ideal to turn into a carpet barn, so when he retired I converted it into one. The pool-hall business wasn't a great business in those days because people in Ireland were very poor at the time.

I've been in the business for the past 40 years. I started out with a carpet shop and now I have a big distribution business that does $100 million a year, with two manufacturing plants, one making carpet and the other making yarn to weave the carpets.

*You buy the wool and make it into the yarn that you use to weave the carpets. Sheep herding is big in Ireland, I hear.*

Yes, there are 12 million sheep in Ireland and only 4.8 million people. Agriculture is still a big business, but the Irish economy in general has been absolutely booming in the last five years. Ireland is the I/T (information/technology) center of Europe. We have had the biggest growth rate in GNP (gross national profit) in the world for the past five or six years, averaging 10 percent every year. So, Ireland has become a very successful country to live in, and a very expensive one to live in. There is a huge pressure on property, on houses. The one thing that Ireland was renowned for the past 150 years was emigration, people leaving the country. Now we're seeing immigration back into the country, up to 150,000 people a year moving to Ireland. At this moment there are unbelievable opportunities in Ireland.

*Did you go to college to prepare yourself for your business?*

Yes, I did. I went to the local primary schools and then to an all-Irish school where we didn't speak English. We studied every subject through the medium of Irish, which basically is a dead language just as Latin, so I had to become very proficient in it. That was a waste of time. Irish still is spoken in some of the smaller parts of Ireland, but in the early '50s the big thing was to try to revive the language and I was one of the victims. I left college at 17 and didn't go on to university.

*Are your daughters involved in the business?*

My oldest daughter is a qualified barrister. In Ireland a lawyer does the research and a barrister presents the case in court, whereas in the United States a lawyer can do both. Although she is a qualified barrister, she has her own carpet distribution company. She began by working for me part-time and then decided to start her own business.

My second daughter owns a taxi company, which now is a deregulated business. If Terry were alive now, he would be destroyed over the deregulation because he had taxi plates that were worth $80,000 a piece last year before deregulation. You used to have to buy a taxi plate in order to run a taxi, but since they've deregulated the business, you can get them for practically nothing.

*Do you play most of your poker during the World Series?*

Yes, 90 percent of it and I only play the satellites and the tournaments. I haven't either the patience or the ability at the moment to play cash games.

*It seems that playing tournaments would require more patience than playing in ring games.*

Perhaps, but the big tournament (the $10,000 buy-in no-limit hold'em event) is the only one that I play. The first year that I got to the final table, I think there were 180 people in the tournament. Now we're talking about having more than 600 people in it. The prize at the end is worthwhile being a little patient for.

*I assume that if you did play cash games, you would play ones with substantial stakes?*

Yes, but first I would have to learn how to play them. I actually don't know how to play cash games.

*If, as you say, you don't play poker all that well, Noel, how did it happen that you won the championship event? You must've done something right.*

When something gets my full attention, I give it my complete concentration. Initially, while most people are playing very tight, I play very loose in the competitions to try to get a decent amount of chips. So I'm either out very early or I'm there with a chance. If I can arrive at the final table, I've found some more chances to win.

*Did you gamble a little bit at the final table?*

Not much gamble, no, but I think that my reading of the players at the final table was excellent. I felt that I could hold my own, even with the likes of Erik Seidel and Huck Seed, whom I believe are superb players. They are much steadier and are more likely to get to the last table than I am.

*But once you get there, you can play with them.*

Actually, I'd love to see a World Series every month. I appreciate all that the Binions have done for the World Series of Poker, making it a high point on my calendar. A $10,000 tournament every month—now *that* would have my full attention—and I feel that then I would have a chance of getting into their league.

*Sure, because you would have more practice. As it is, you don't practice playing poker very often.*

No, and unfortunately when I play in a satellite, I'm doing all sorts of wild things because it doesn't matter as much to me.

*You need a very big carrot at the end of the stick?*

That's the long and the short of it. I'd love to have ten of those carrots every year.

*You don't play any game except no-limit hold'em and only the World Series, with the exception of the Irish tournaments?*

That's why I'm not a good subject for a magazine article—I'm not a professional poker player.

*You don't need to be a professional player to be a world champion. You have the appearance, the decorum and the manners that represent the poker world best.*

No one has better manners than Erik Seidel.

*You seem to feel comfortable here in the States, but after you won the championship were you uncomfortable with all the media attention? Was everyone accosting you for interviews and photographs, the whole nine yards?*

Yes, I feel very comfortable here and yes they did. I think I've become somewhat of a recluse over the past eight or nine years. Basically I'm a shy person. I like people, but I don't like to be probed. The easy way out is to keep to myself. I've never had a business card in my life. I've never had an answering machine on my phone. It's just a thing called privacy.

*Not even a cell phone?*

I did buy a mobile phone when they first came out, when they were very expensive. And I found that I was having to make every decision in the business because nobody would make a decision unless they called me first. And that wasn't what I was paying them for. Whether it would be white or pink toilet paper—it was getting down to that stage—so I got rid of the phone.

*You're quite an equestrian enthusiast, so to speak.*

Yes, I keep a few horses (laughing). I train horses for myself as well. Thoroughbreds. I have just bought a new place with stables and I'm doing it up at this moment.

*Actually, you've been written about in two of Raymond Smith's books that are popular in Ireland: "High Rollers of the Turf" and "Better One Day as a Lion." He mentioned that you are "famous for (your) 4-million-pound double bid at Cheltendam in '91." I gather that you bet the horses as well as breed them?*

Well, you know, you have to keep busy. I suppose that's the gambler in me. I also see how my biggest fame comes from gambling, that's fairly obvious—and as long as I control it within reason, I can live with it.

*Self-control is important in almost anything, isn't it?*

Yes. Oscar Wilde, the famous Irish playwright, once said that he reckoned that he could control everything except temptation.


"No-limit hold'em is hours of boredom and moments of sheer terror."

— Tom McEvoy


"Limit poker is a science, but no-limit is an art. In limit, you are shooting at a target. In no-limit, the target comes alive and shoots back at you."

— Crandall Addington

1973 World Champion Walter Clyde "Puggy" Pearson in one of the many colorful costumes he has worn over the years at the World Series of Poker.

The reigning World Champion, Chris Ferguson (l), congratulates his successor, 2001 World Poker Champion, Carlos Mortensen.

World Champions of Poker (l to r) Doyle Brunson, Bobby Baldwin, Johnny Chan, Amarillo Slim Preston and Brad Daugherty pose for photographer Larry Grossman at the 1998 World Series of Poker.

# 2000 World Championship Event
## 31st World Series of Poker
### Number of Entries: 512

────────── The Championship Table ──────────

| The Finalists | Chip Count | Hometown |
|---|---|---|
| Roman Abinsay | $521,000 | Stockton, CA |
| Mickey Appleman | Finished 9th | New York, NY |
| T.J. Cloutier | $216,000 | Richardson, TX |
| Chris Ferguson | $2,853,000 | Pacific Palisades, CA |
| Tom Franklin | Finished 8th | Gulfport, MS |
| Hasan Habib | $464,000 | Bell Gardens, CA |
| Steve Kaufman | $511,000 | Cincinnati, OH |
| Jim McManus | $554,000 | Kenilworth, IL |
| Jeff Shulman | Finished 7th | Las Vegas, NV |

──────────── The Last Hand ────────────

**Ferguson's Cards**          **Cloutier's Cards**

_____ Flop _____ Turn _____ River

| The Finish | Prize Money |
|------------|-------------|
| 1st Ferguson | $ 1,500,000 |
| 2nd Cloutier | $ 896,000 |
| 3rd Kaufman | $ 570,500 |
| 4th Habib | $ 326,000 |
| 5th McManus | $ 247,760 |
| 6th Abinsay | $ 195,600 |
| 7th Shulman | $ 146,700 |
| 8th Franklin | $ 97,800 |
| 9th Appleman | $ 74,980 |

## How It Happened
### by T.J. Cloutier

When we started the final table, Chris Ferguson had a lot of chips, the four others were close in chip count with $400,000 or more, and I had $216,000. When I got up that morning, I formed a plan that I explained to my wife: "I'll let them knock each other out and try to get heads up with Chris." I thought that if my plan worked, I'd get to play heads up with Chris because of the amount of chips he had to start with. Seeing that I believe that poker is a game of mistakes, I wanted to let the others make the mistakes themselves to put me in a position where I had a chance to win. They were all fine players, but none of them were experienced in final table play except Chris. That's why I thought they would make major errors in crucial spots—and as it came up, that's exactly what happened. They dropped like flies.

The key element for me in this championship play was that when we started playing heads up, Chris had $4,700,000 in chips and I had $400,000 and I took the lead away from him. Never at any time did I get my money in with the worst hand. I kept chipping away at him, meaning that I was trying to get Chris to take me off in certain spots, which he did. If I flopped a set and checked to him, it seemed that he would always catch some card that he thought was good enough to call with. When I had the best hand I tried to let him pay, but not enough that it would make him drop his hand because I wanted to get paid on all those hands, that's what chipping away means.

I could see that he was getting worried, and I thought there might be a chance that he was going to miscalculate the value of a hand—and he did when he called my all-in bet with A-9 when I held A-Q. But luck is a part of poker, and he caught a nine on the river that won the title for him. The way that he explained it made sense to me—he said he thought that on that one day, he couldn't beat me if we just played out the hands. He thought that he had to beat me in a major pot, so he just decided to go with the hand. Obviously Chris thought that if he caught an ace, he'd have a hand, but he was in horrible position. The interesting part is that it was his nine kicker that made his hand a winner, not the ace. And you know what? I saw that nine coming before the dealer ever peeled it off. It was as though I was looking right through the deck.

## Highlights

2000 was the first year that the no-limit finale attracted a field of more than 500 players—in all the tournaments, there were more than 4,000 entries with $14,500,000 in prize money to be won. As an added attraction, the 2000 WSOP paid a record $1,500,000 to the winner of the championship event. It wasn't the first time that T.J. Cloutier was the runner-up: In 1985 he placed second to his good friend Bill Smith. For winner Chris Ferguson, however, it was a fabulous first as he turned his premier final-table appearance into "a million and change."

Arriving at the championship table in last chip position, Cloutier fought an uphill battle to set up the final confrontation against chip leader Ferguson, who received approximately 34 percent of the prize pool of $5,112,000 for winning the championship.

"Cloutier is known as an instinctive player with decades of experience who can expertly read his opponents. He treats poker as a job. Ferguson approaches poker as an academic pursuit and says the gambling aspect of the game holds little appeal for him."
— Anne Colby in *The Los Angeles Times*

"I thought there was a very small chance that I had the best hand. And if I had the best hand, I was giving up a lot more by folding."
— Chris Ferguson to reporter Anne Colby on why he called T.J. Cloutier's all-in bet in the final hand of the 2000 WSOP

# Chris Ferguson
## A Champ Who Waltzes in Three Worlds
### Interview with a Champ (1998) by Dana Smith

I caught up with Chris Ferguson at the 1998 World Series of Poker, but I could just as easily have run into him on the dance floor or in the halls of academe. He's one well-rounded guy, this man whose nickname is "Jesus." With his long wavy hair, well-groomed beard and polite demeanor, Ferguson possesses that rare attribute called "presence." Not long after our interview, Ferguson earned a Ph.D. degree at U.C.L.A. with a major in computer science (artificial intelligence), but this computer Merlin also works his wizardry on the tournament circuit and makes mambo magic on the dance floor.

Two years after I wrote this interview, Ferguson won the championship event at the 2000 World Series of Poker in a classic draw-out against runner-up T.J. Cloutier which has since become a widely discussed hand. Their confrontation at the final table probably will go down as one of the greatest heads-up matches in WSOP history. Prior to winning the championship event that year, Ferguson won the seven-card stud championship, and went on to win his third WSOP bracelet in 2001 for Omaha high-low. Not only is he respected for his tournament prowess—through 2002 he had $2,147,652 at the WSOP—Ferguson also is recognized as one of the nicest people in the poker world.

Although the erudite Ferguson is far from synthetic, we began by discussing artificial intelligence "The basic idea of all artificial intelligence is to get computers to perform tasks that humans are considered to be good at," he explained. "Vision is one of them. You can put a picture on the computer screen, but it's very difficult for the computer to determine whether the image is a table, a cup, or a poker chip. That is still one very difficult problem in computer science. Another one is language recognition—to be able to speak into a computer, have it write your words on the screen *and* have some understanding of the meaning of those words. Accomplishing these tasks would be typical of artificial intelligence. More trivial tasks may be things such as playing poker."

*There are some voice recognition programs on the shelves today, but computer scientists hope to take them one step farther into understanding what you're saying?*

"Understanding" may be too strong—it's quite difficult to find a word to express the concept. There are different degrees of understanding. For example, it's quite easy for a computer to look up a word in the dictionary and find its definition—the hard part is putting a word in a context and understanding its meaning within that context.

*Sometimes, even we humans have that problem! What are you hoping to accomplish with your Ph.D. degree?*

Eventually I plan to work for a company on Wall Street, analyzing stocks or trading.

*Do you also use the computer for poker practice?*

Poker is just a sideline with me, and I play it more for the challenge than the money. But yes, I do a lot of work with poker on the computer. I analyze situations, trying to simplify the game by making certain assumptions and then solving them to arrive at some basic rules that are useful in natural play.

*You've been very successful in tournaments. Have some of your computer generated rules helped you?*

Absolutely. I don't have a lot of time to spend at poker since that isn't what I do for a living, so I decided to primarily play tournaments because I felt that the competition in them would be the greatest. I figure that the way to learn to play better is to play against the top players—I learn best by playing against the best.

*I first saw you play last year at the final table of the WSOP $2,000 pot-limit hold'em event. I couldn't help but notice your fine play against such notables as Tom McEvoy, David Ulliott (the winner), Chris Truby and Eskimo Clark. A few days later at the $3,000 no-limit hold'em event that Max Stern eventually won, there you were at the final table again.*

I placed sixth in that pot-limit event and seventh in the no-limit hold'em tournament. But my highest finish at the *WSOP* came a few days ago when I placed fourth in the $2,000 pot-limit hold'em tournament, which was kind of disappointing.

*That wouldn't be disappointing to a lot of other people!*

I understand that and I'm not unhappy with my overall performance. It's just that I've made it to the final table at the WSOP six times and not making it once to the top three is disappointing.

*Still, you've made a good name and some money for yourself at poker. What do you do for your primary income?*

I am a research assistant and I've also done consulting work for the California State lottery and the Bureau of the Census, as well as for individuals. Of course, I also make a decent amount of money at gambling, although that isn't my primary focus.

*How did you get into gambling?*

Even back in the fourth grade, I was playing poker and in high school we played it a lot. Early in my college career, I took occasional trips to Las Vegas where I played $1-$2 and $2-$4 games. By playing very tightly, waiting for extremely good hands, I found that I could make $4 an hour. I played for the challenge, to see if I could make a living at poker, and if you call $4 an hour a living, I discovered that I could do it.

*And then you made a jump?*

Yes, but first there's another part to my background: My father, Thomas, teaches statistics and game theory at U.C.L.A., so when I was young we always played games in our home. He continually analyzed games or invented new ones, so I grew up with a very strong background in gamesmanship. My mother also has a Ph.D. in mathematics, specializing in the field of topology.

*Sounds as though you come by your game skills naturally— maybe it's in your genes?*

I don't think there are any genes specific to playing poker (laughing). Of course, Jack Keller and his daughter, Kathy Kolberg, and Doyle and Todd Brunson, may prove me wrong on this one.

*How did you go about stepping up to higher limits?*

I came into a large amount of money by winning a big blackjack tournament. At that point, I said "Well, I've made some money here, so now I can expand." I never expected to make money instantly at poker, of course, especially since I hadn't been playing against the best opponents (I apologize to my high school friends for saying this.)

*There are no champions among your high school buds?*

Not yet. Anyway, I knew that since I hadn't been playing at a very high level it would take me a while to hone my skills.

*You must've sharpened up quite a bit: You won a big one at the Legends of Poker.*

I won the $300 no-limit hold'em event at the Legends and I've also taken titles in about five other tournaments, including one or two in lowball. I've also been pretty successful in the best all-around player finals, placing second at the Legends last year and second in the best all-around playoffs the year before. I won a car for that finish.

*Now let's change the music and waltz over to your other interest, dancing.*

I've been dancing for about nine years and ran the U.C.L.A. ballroom dance club for three years. I do all the ballroom dances—the foxtrot, waltz, tango, mambo. But these days I mostly dance the West Coast Swing, the latest form of swing dance. If you've ever watched "Happy Days," you know what the swing was like in the '50s.

*Hey, Chris, I lived the '50s!*

Well, the swing is still a living dance—it changes all the time—as opposed to some of the ballroom dances that are somewhat old and aren't done socially as much anymore. You meet great people dancing the swing.

*Is dancing a good way to keep in physical shape?*

I guess it helps, although I don't consider dancing to be getting a lot of exercise. I used to play basketball and volleyball, pick-up games—now *that* was a lot of exercise. But my body got too beat up and I don't play much any more. Dancing is a totally different world than poker, although I do know some great players who dance. Mike Sexton, for example, is an excellent dancer and used to teach dance.

I've competed in some dance contests, mostly Jack and Jill events in which men and women enter the event individually. Your dance partner is selected at random, so that you don't know ahead of time who you'll be dancing with or what the music will be. You can improvise and it's a lot of fun. I've also competed on dance teams and there you must be very precise. There might be eight couples on the team doing a single routine to the same song and you are judged in part on your degree of synchronization.

*Seeing you around the poker world, one gets a different impression of you than the "real" Chris Ferguson. With that hair, the black clothes and black Western hat, you look like one of the desperadoes in the old movies. What's with the garb?*

What are you saying here, that I look like a long-haired bum?! Seriously, it's part of an image for poker. Outside the poker world, I never wear a cowboy hat. Without it, I may look more like a university professor than a poker player. It's nice to have the image of being a good poker player, but some people think that they want the image of *not* being a good player, believing that the opposition will try to outplay them and they can take advantage of that. In poker, there seems to be a lot of misdirection. For example, players who don't know me may think, "That guy wears a cowboy hat. He probably plays a lot of poker but he doesn't understand the mathematics behind it." (I apologize to those cowboys who *do* understand the math.) That perception of me would be dead wrong.

*You're right about that! Comments about poker?*

Some people might think that there is one basic way to play poker, but there isn't. There are many different styles of play. Two people may be dealt the same hand, play it quite differently, and yet both will be successful. In tournament poker, you have to have a long attention span, be very concentrated, be aware of what's going on, and remain very focused.

*You seem to waltz quite smoothly in your three worlds.*

Yes, and I enjoy them all although there is very little crossover among them. When you take up something new, you have to give up something old. I guess I'm partly trying to fill the void that was left when I stopped playing sports.

"Carlos Mortensen had the remaining players lining up to get off that table, he had them bursting into tears in relief when they finally got busted out, they were so happy to get out from the glare."
— Jesse May upon viewing the 2001 WSOP

"I don't care who you are or how good you are, when you won your last tournament, you were very lucky." — Tom McEvoy

# 2001 World Championship Event
## 32nd World Series of Poker
### Number of Entries: 613

────────── The Championship Table ──────────

| The Finalists | Chip Count | Hometown |
| --- | --- | --- |
| Phil Gordon | $681,000 | South Tahoe, CA |
| Phil Hellmuth, Jr. | $859,000 | Palo Alto, CA |
| John Inashima | $328,000 | Pasadena, CA |
| Mike Matusow | $767,000 | Henderson, NV |
| Carlos Mortensen | $873,000 | Madrid, Spain |
| Henry Nowakowski | $1,076,000 | Frankfurt, Germany |
| Steve Riehle | $407,000 | Lompoc, CA |
| Stan Schrier | $672,000 | Omaha, NB |
| Dewey Tomko | $467,000 | Haines City, FL |

──────────── The Last Hand ────────────

**Mortensen's Cards**      **Tomko's Cards**

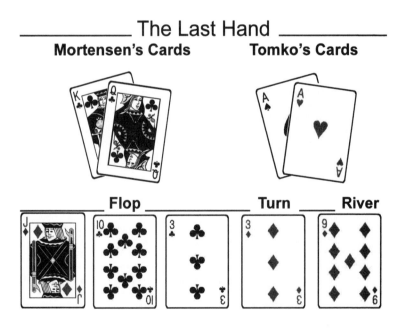

Flop ──────────── Turn ──── River

| The Finish | Prize Money |
|---|---|
| 1st Mortensen | $1,500,000 |
| 2nd Tomko | $1,098,925 |
| 3rd Schrier | $ 699,315 |
| 4th Gordon | $ 399,610 |
| 5th Hellmuth | $ 303,705 |
| 6th Matusow | $ 239,765 |
| 7th Nowakowski | $ 179,825 |
| 8th Riehle | $ 119,885 |
| 9th Inashima | $ 91,910 |

## How It Happened

With a 2-to-1 chip lead over Dewey Tomko, a Florida golf course owner and professional poker player, Spanish poker whiz Carlos Mortensen raised to $100,000 before the flop with the K♣ Q♣. Tomko flat-called with pocket aces in an apparent attempt to trap Mortensen. The flop gave Tomko an overpair and Mortensen draws to a straight and a flush. Again he bet $100,000, but this time Tomko raised $400,000. Mortensen then moved in all his chips and Tomko called with his remaining $1.5 million. The 9♦ on the river gave Mortensen the winning straight, the WSOP title, and $1.5 million in cash. Mortensen gained his entry into the championship event by winning the Shooting Stars championship at Bay 101 in San Jose, California, one month earlier. Mortensen's WSOP winnings through 2002 totaled $1,563,515. Tomko has won $1,915,644.

## Highlights

For the first time, the WSOP championship event lasted five days, and all nine finalists were filmed for the video of the championship table. For the second time Dewey Tomko was the runner-up. His other second-place finish came in 1982 against Jack Straus.

Stu "The Kid" Ungar was posthumously inducted into the Poker Hall of Fame. Ungar, who died in 1998 at the age of 45, was the only three-time champion who played against a full field of players. Johnny Moss was elected for the title in 1970, and defeated a total of around 40 opponents in his other two victories. Ungar defeated 72 opponents in 1980, 74 in 1981 and 311 in 1997.

# 2002 World Championship Event
## 33rd World Series of Poker
### Number of Entries: 631

## ——— The Championship Table ———

| The Finalists | Chip Count | Hometown |
|---|---|---|
| Tony D (Tam Duong) | $231,000 | Los Angeles, CA |
| Julian Gardner | $394,000 | Manchester, UK |
| Scott Gray | $545,000 | Dublin, Ireland |
| Harley Hall | $161,000 | Capistrano, CA |
| Minh Ly | $614,000 | Las Vegas, NV |
| Ralph Perry | $766,000 | Las Vegas, NV |
| Russell Rosenblum | $927,000 | Bethesda, MD |
| John Shipley | $2,033,000 | Solihull, UK |
| Robert Varkonyi | $640,000 | Brooklyn, NY |

## ——————— The Last Hand ———————

### Varkonyi's Cards    Gardner's Cards

### ———— Flop ———————— Turn ——— River

| The Finish | Prize Money |
|---|---|
| 1st Varkonyi | $ 2,000,000 |
| 2nd Gardner | $ 1,100,000 |
| 3rd Perry | $   550,000 |
| 4th Gray | $   281,400 |
| 5th Hall | $   195,000 |
| 6th Rosenblum | $   150,000 |
| 7th Shipley | $   120,000 |
| 8th Duong | $   100,000 |
| 9th Ly | $    85,000 |

## How It Happened

With the blinds at $20,000-$40,000 and an ante of $5,000, semi-retired investment banker Robert Varkonyi bet $90,000 before the flop with Q-10, a hand that had won several big pots for him earlier. Julian Gardner, a British professional poker player, called with the J♣ 8♣. The flop gave Varkonyi top pair and Gardner a flush draw. Gardner checked, Varkonyi bet $50,000 and Gardner moved all in with his remaining $765,000 in chips. Varkonyi called. If Gardner won the hand, his stack would rise to about $1.5 million and put him back in the race with a 3-to-1 chip deficit. Indeed Gardner made the flush when the 10♣ fell on the river, but to no avail as it also gave Varkonyi the winning full house—plus $2,000,000 prize money.

## Highlights

The tournament schedule, designed by 1983 World Champion Tom McEvoy, included 35 preliminary tournaments, including four new events—gold bracelet match play, H.O.R.S.E., triple draw lowball, and half limit hold'em/half seven-card stud. The total prize money for all events was $19,599,230. For the first time in WSOP history, the first prize in the title match was $2,000,000, approximately 31 percent of the prize pool of $6,310,000. Lyle Berman and Johnny Chan were inducted into the Poker Hall of Fame.

"Poker may have been the most important thing I learned at MIT. That week I was in the zone—absolutely focused and centered and, of course, lucky." — 1983 MIT graduate Robert Varkonyi to journalist Darren J. Clarke on winning the 2002 WSOP championship

# 2003 World Championship Event
## 34rd World Series of Poker
### Number of Entries: 839

## —————— The Championship Table ——————

| The Finalists | Chip Count | Hometown |
| --- | --- | --- |
| Tomer Benvenisti | $922,000 | Las Vegas, NV |
| Sam Farha | $999,000 | Houston, TX |
| David Grey | $338,000 | Henderson, NV |
| Dan Harrington | $574,000 | Santa Monica, CA |
| Jason Lester | $695,000 | Las Vegas, NV |
| Chris Moneymaker | $2,344,000 | Spring Hill, TN |
| Young Pak | $360,000 | Bainbridge, WA |
| David Singer | $750,000 | Mamaroneck, NY |
| Amir Vahedi | $1,407,000 | Reseda, CA |

## —————— The Last Hand ——————

**Moneymaker's Cards**        **Farha's Cards**

**Flop** _____ **Turn** _____ **River**

## The Finish Prize Money

| The Finish | | Prize Money |
|---|---|---|
| 1st | Moneymaker | $ 2,500,000 |
| 2nd | Farha | $ 1,300,000 |
| 3rd | Harrington | $ 650,000 |
| 4th | Lester | $ 440,000 |
| 5th | Benvenisti | $ 320,000 |
| 6th | Vahedi | $ 250,000 |
| 7th | Pak | $ 200,000 |
| 8th | Grey | $ 160,000 |
| 9th | Singer | $ 120,000 |

## How It Happened

Chris Moneymaker, an accountant who won his entry into the tournament via an online satellite, and Sam Farha, a high-stakes gambler from Texas, started playing heads-up no-limit hold'em for all the marbles at the championship table with Moneymaker in the lead by $5,490,000 in chips to Farha's $2,900,000. After sparring with Farha for 20 hands, Moneymaker moved in with all his chips during a key hand, winning a huge pot that put him further in the lead by $6.6 million to $1.8 million. In the last hand, Farha (holding J-10) raised to $100,000 from the small blind. Moneymaker called with 5-4. On the J-5-4 flop, Moneymaker checked his two pair and Farha bet $175,000 with top pair. Moneymaker raised $275,000, Farha moved in with all his chips, and Moneymaker called. A full house on the river gave the novice tournament player a record payday of $2.5 million, the gold bracelet, and the 2003 World Championship of Poker. Farha's consolation prize was a mere $1,300,000.

## Highlights

Playing in the biggest field ever at the WSOP, Moneymaker's win was all the more newsworthy because he became the first online satellite winner to go on to win the Big One. An overnight celebrity, Moneymaker appeared on the David Letterman Show and others. But as tournament reporter Andrew N.S. Glazer wrote, "The win is probably even bigger for online poker. Millions of people who didn't know that online poker existed are now going to hear a lot about it." Bobby Baldwin, the 1978 World Champion of Poker and CEO of Mirage Resorts, was inducted into the Poker Hall of Fame.

The 1997 Championship Table. Champion Stu Ungar (l) and runner-up John Strzemp. The championship table was televised on an elevated stage on Fremont Street in Downtown Las Vegas. Television star Gabe Kaplan announced the event, along with veteran WSOP tournament director Jim Albrecht, who died in 2003.

The 1998 Championship Table. Kevin McBride (l), the runner-up; T.J. Cloutier, who finished third; and champion Scotty Nguyen.

The 1999 Championship Table. Clockwise from dealer's left: Erik Seidel, who finished fourth; Huck Seed, sixth place; champion Noel Furlong; and Padraig Parkinson, who finished third.

The 2000 Championship Table. Champion Chris Ferguson (l) and runner-up T.J. Cloutier.

# Index of Players and Personalities

# Photographic Credits

*Copyright University of Nevada—Las Vegas, 2003*
Page 28, Amarillo Slim Preston
Page 31, Preston, Moss & Binion
Pages 42-43, 1974 WSOP
Page 47, Doyle Brunson
Pages 58-59, 1976 WSOP
Page 107, 1976 WSOP

*Courtesy of the Las Vegas*
*News Bureau*
Page 19, Johnny Moss
Page 41, Johnny Moss
Page 76, Doyle Brunson

*Courtesy of Larry Grossman*
Pages 33 & 39, Puggy Pearson
Page 76, Stu Ungar
Page 77, Johnny Chan
Page 99, Ten WSOP champions
Page 107, 1993 WSOP
Pages 111 & 113, Johnny Chan
Page 114, Erik Seidel
Page 118, Mansour Matloubi
Page 127, Hamid Dastmalchi
Page 129, Jim Bechtel
Page 131, Russ Hamilton
Page 137, Dan Harrington
Page 143, 1994 WSOP
Page 145, Huck Seed
Page 147, Stu Ungar
Page 153, Scotty Nguyen
Page 155, Noel Furlong
Page 163, 3 Photos of champions
Page 165, Chris Ferguson
Page 173, Carlos Mortensen
Page 175, Robert Varkonyi
Page 177, Chris Moneymaker
Page 178, 179, 1997 & 1998 WSOP
Page 180, 181, 1999 & 2000 WSOP

# References

**Books**

The Biggest Game in Town, A. Alvarez, Houghton Mifflin Company, Boston, 1983.

Fast Company, Jon Bradshaw, Harper & Row, New York, 1975.

Cowboys, Gamblers & Hustlers, Byron "Cowboy" Wolford, Cardsmith Publishing, Las Vegas, 2002.

**Periodicals**

Card Player magazine, 1988-2003.

"Inside the World Series of Poker," Al Reinert, Texas Monthly, August, 1973.

"Pythagorus, Pi and Pluck at Vegas' Poker World," Anne Colby, Los Angeles Times, May 26, 2001.

"Ungar's Play Was as Hot as the Gallery," Ed Koch and Gary Thompson, Las Vegas Sun, May 16, 1997.

"Known for Poker Prowess, Ungar Had Deeper Side," Ed Koch, Las Vegas Sun, November 27, 1998.

"When It Came to Everyday Life, Poker Champ Was Just a Kid," John L. Smith, Las Vegas Review Journal, November 24, 1998.

"Troubled Card Genius Stu Ungar Couldn't Win Win the Game of Life," Brad Reagan, Las Vegas Life, May, 2002."

"Famed Gambler Ungar Dies at 45," Ed Koch, Las Vegas Sun, November 23, 1998.

"Poker-Playing Alum Knows When to Hold'em," Darren J. Clarke, Tech Talk (MIT News Office), August 14, 2002.

"From $40 to Moneymaker," by Jeff Simpson, Las Vegas Review Journal, May 25, 2003.

## Internet Resources

www.thepokerforum.com, "Poker Hall of Fame."

www.playwinningpoker.com, "WSOP Winners, 1970-2000."

www.entertainmenttonight (ET Online), "The World Series of Poker—Matt Damon & Ed Norton," May 12, 1998.

www.binions.com, "World Series Boasts Colorful History."

www.thegoodgamblingguide.co.uk, "Day Five WSOP-Day of Yeah!" Jesse May; and "Stu Ungar (1953-1998) The Tortured Champion."

www.freespace.virgin.net, "Four Days, Three Million Dollars, The WSOP, Las Vegas," three extracts from an article in London Evening Standard and Total Sport, Ben Oliver, August, 1997.

www.pokerpages.com, "Poker Greats: Stu Ungar," Mike Sexton.

www.CasinoGaming.com, "World Series of Poker 2003" compiled by Nolan Dalla

www.bettingsearch.com, "The Chris Moneymaker Story."

Noted gaming photographer Larry Grossman with Johnny Moss.

# About the Authors

## Dana Smith

Dana Smith is the owner of Cardsmith Publishing and the author of several poker books using her son's name, Shane Smith. She began writing for Card Player magazine in 1990, interviewing more than 100 poker champions for her column, "Interview with a Champ." Smith has an M.A. degree from Cal State University and was in business in California before moving to Las Vegas to enter the poker world.

## Tom McEvoy

Tom McEvoy won the World Series of Poker in 1983 a few days after winning the limit hold'em title. One of the most recognizable people in the poker world, McEvoy is the author of 7 poker books and has been a Card Player columnist for 15 years. He earned a B.S. degree in accounting from Ferris State University and was an accountant for 12 years before moving to Las Vegas to seek his fortune as a professional poker player.

## Ralph Wheeler

Ralph Wheeler is a recreational poker player and World Series of Poker buff. After earning a B.F.A. degree from Ohio State, he joined General Electric where he was the Exhibit and Special Events Manager. When he retired, Wheeler began a new career as a cartoonist. He is the author of "The Wacky Side of Poker" and two calendars for poker players.

# Gallery of Champions

1970-'71-'74
Johnny Moss

1972
Amarillo Slim
Preston

1973
Puggy Pearson

1975
Brian "Sailor"
Roberts

1976-1977
Doyle "Texas
Dolly" Brunson

1978
Bobby Baldwin

1979
Hal Fowler

1980-81-97
Stu "The Kid"
Ungar

1982
Jack Straus

1983
Tom McEvoy

1984
Jack Keller

1985
Bill Smith

1986
Berry Johnston

1987-88
Johnny Chan

1989
Phil Hellmuth

1990
Mansour
Matloubi

1991
Brad
Daugherty

1992
Hamid
Dastmalchi

1993
Jim
Bechtel

1994
Russ
Hamilton

1995
Dan Harrington

1996
Huck Seed

1998
Scotty
Nguyen

1999
Noel Furlong

2000
Chris
Ferguson

2001
Carlos
Mortensen

2002
Robert
Varkonyi

2003
Chris
Moneymaker

# GREAT POKER BOOKS
## ADD THESE TO YOUR LIBRARY - ORDER NOW!

**WINNER'S GUIDE TO TEXAS HOLD' EM POKER** by Ken Warren - The most comprehensive book on beating hold 'em shows serious players how to play every hand from every position with every type of flop. Learn the 14 categories of starting hands, the 10 most common Hold'em tells, how to evaluate a game for profit, value of deception, art of bluffing, 8 secrets to winning, starting hand categories, position, more! Bonus: Includes detailed analysis of the top 40 hands and the most complete chapter on hold'em odds in print. Over 50,000 copies in print. 224 pages, 5 1/2 x 8 1/2, paperback, $14.95.

**KEN WARREN TEACHES TEXAS HOLD 'EM** by Ken Warren - This is a step-by-step comprehensive manual for making money at hold 'em poker. 42 powerful chapters teach you one lesson at a time. Great practical advice and concepts with examples from actual games and how to apply them to your own play. Lessons include: Starting Cards, Playing Position, Raising, Check-raising, Tells, Game/Seat Selection, Dominated Hands, Odds, much more. This book is already a huge fan favorite and best-seller! 416 pgs. $26.95

**WINNER'S GUIDE TO OMAHA POKER** by Ken Warren - In a concise and easy-to-understand style, Warren shows beginning and intermediate Omaha players how to win from the first time they play. You'll learn the rules, betting and blind structure, why to play Omaha, the advantages of Omaha over Texas Hold'em, glossary, reading the board, basic strategies, Omaha high, Omaha hi-low split 8/better, how to play draws and made hands, evaluation of starting hands, counting outs, computing pot odds, the unique characteristics of split-pot games, the best and worst Omaha hands, how to play before the flop, how to play on the flop, how to play on the turn and river and much more. 224 pgs. $19.95

**POKER WISDOM OF A CHAMPION** by Doyle Brunson - Learn what it takes to be a great poker player by climbing inside the mind of poker's most famous champion. Fascinating anecdotes and adventures from Doyle's early career playing poker in roadhouses and with other great champions are interspersed with lessons one can learn from the champion who has made more money at poker than anyone else in the history of the game. Readers learn what makes a great player tick, how he approaches the game, and receive candid, powerful advice from the legend himself. The Mad Genius of poker, Mike Caro, says, "Brunson is the greatest poker player who ever lived . This book shows why." 192 pgs. $14.95.

**POKER TOURNAMENT TIPS FROM THE PROS** by Shane Smith - Essential advice from poker theorists, authors, and tournament winners on the best strategies for winning the big prizes at low-limit re-buy tournaments. Learn the best strategies for each of the four stages of play—opening, middle, late and final—how to avoid 26 potential traps, advice on re-buys, aggressive play, clock-watching, inside moves, top 20 tips for winning tournaments, more. Advice from McEvoy, Caro, Malmuth, Ciaffone, others. 160 pages, 5 1/2 x 8 1/2, $19.95.

**HOW TO WIN AT OMAHA HIGH-LOW POKER** by Mike Cappelletti - Clearly written strategies and powerful advice shows the essential winning strategies for beating the hottest new casino poker game—Omaha high-low poker! This money-making guide includes more than sixty hard-hitting sections on Omaha. Players learn the rules of play, best starting hands, strategies for the flop, turn, and river, how to read the board for both high and low, dangerous draws, and how to beat low-limit tournaments. Includes odds charts, glossary, low-limit tips, strategic ideas. 304 pgs, $19.95.

# GREAT POKER BOOKS
## ADD THESE TO YOUR LIBRARY - ORDER NOW!

**HOW TO BEAT LOW LIMIT 7 CARD STUD POKER** by Paul Kammen - Written for low limit and first time players, you'll learn the different hands that can be played, the correct bets to make, and how to tailor strategies for maximum profits. Tons of information includes spread-limit and fixed-limit game, starting hands, 3rd-7th street strategy, overcards, psychology and much more. 192 pgs. $14.95.

**OMAHA HI-LO POKER** by Shane Smith - Learn essential winning strategies for beating Omaha high-low; the best starting hands, how to play the flop, turn, and river, how to read the board for both high and low, dangerous draws, and how to win low-limit tournaments. Smith shows the differences between Omaha high-low and hold'em strategies. Includes odds charts, glossary, low-limit tips, strategic ideas. 84 pages, 8 x 11, spiral bound, $17.95.

**7-CARD STUD (THE COMPLETE COURSE IN WINNING AT MEDIUM & LOWER LIMITS)** by Roy West - Learn the latest strategies for winning at $1-$4 spread-limit up to $10-$20 fixed-limit games. Covers starting hands, 3rd-7th street strategy for playing most hands, overcards, selective aggressiveness, reading hands, secrets of the pros, psychology, more - in a 42 "lesson" informal format. Includes bonus chapter on 7-stud tournament strategy by World Champion Tom McEvoy. 160 pages, paperback, $24.95.

**WINNING LOW LIMIT HOLD'EM** by Lee Jones - This essential book on playing 1-4, 3-6, and 1-4-8-8 low limit hold'em is packed with insights on winning: pre-flop positional play; playing the flop in all positions with a pair, two pair, trips, overcards, draws, made and nothing hands; turn and river play; how to read the board; avoiding trash hands; using the check-raise; bluffing, stereotypes, much more. Includes quizzes with answers. Terrific book. 176 pages, 5 1/2 x 8 1/2, paperback, $19.95.

**BOBBY BALDWIN'S WINNING POKER SECRETS** by Mike Caro with Bobby Baldwin. New edition - now back in print! This is the fascinating account of former world champion Bobby Baldwin's early career playing poker in roadhouses and against other poker legends and his meteoric rise to the championship. It is interspersed with important lessons on what makes a great player tick and how he approaches the game. Baldwin and Mike Caro, both of whom are co-authors of the classic Doyle Brunson's Super System, cover the common mistakes average players make at seven poker variations and the dynamic winning concepts they must employ to win. Endorsed by poker legends and superstars Doyle Brunson and Amarillo Slim. 256 pages, 5 1/2 x 8 1/2, paperback, $14.95.

**HANDBOOK OF WINNING POKER** by Edwin Silberstang - Beginner's book to poker explains the basics of more than 10 casino and home poker games including variations of hold'em, draw, stud, lowball, high-low, more. Special chapters cover games in California, Nevada, world championship play, bluffing, the psychology of winning, and how to get the winning edge. Paperback. 160 pgs, $9.95.

**WINNING POKER FOR THE SERIOUS PLAYER** by Edwin Silberstang - More than 100 actual examples and tons of advice on beating 7 Card Stud, Texas Hold 'Em, Draw Poker, Loball, High-Low and 10 other variations. Silberstang analyzes the essentials of being a great player; reading tells, analyzing tables, playing position, mastering the art of deception, creating fear at the table. Also, psychological tactics, when to play aggressive or slow play, or fold, expert plays, more. Colorful glossary included. 304 pages, 6 x 9, $16.95.

**HOW TO PLAY WINNING POKER** by Avery Cardoza - New and expanded edition shows playing and winning strategies for all major games: five & seven stud games, omaha, draw poker, hold'em, and high-low, both for home and casino play. You'll learn 15 winning poker concepts, how to minimize losses and maximize profits, how to read opponents and gain the edge against their style, how to use use pot odds, tells, position, more. 160 pgs. $12.95

# FROM CARDSMITH'S EXCITING LIBRARY

## ADD THESE TO YOUR COLLECTION - ORDER NOW!

**COWBOYS, GAMBLERS & HUSTLERS: The True Adventures of a Rodeo Champion & Poker Legend** by Byron "Cowboy" Wolford. Ride along with the road gamblers as they fade the white line from Dallas to Shreveport to Houston in the 1960s in search of a score. Feel the fear and frustration of being hijacked, getting arrested for playing poker, and having to outwit card sharps and scam artists. Wolford survived it all to win a WSOP gold bracelet playing with poker greats Amarillo Slim Preston, Johnny Moss and Bobby Baldwin (and 30 rodeo belt buckles). Read fascinating yarns about life on the rough and tumble, and colorful adventures as a road gambler and hustler gambling in smoky backrooms with legends Titanic Thompson, Jack Straus, Doyle Brunson and get a look at vintage Las Vegas when Cowboy's friend, Benny Binion ruled Glitter Gulch. Read about the most famous bluff in WSOP history. Endorsed by Jack Binion, Doyle Brunson & Bobby Baldwin, who says, Cowboy is probably the best gambling story teller in the world. 304 pages, $19.95.

**SECRETS OF WINNING POKER** by Tex Sheahan. This is a compilation of Sheahan's best articles from 15 years of writing for the major gaming magazines as his legacy to poker players. Sheahan gives you sound advice on winning poker strategies for hold'em and 7-card stud. Chapters on tournament play, psychology, personality profiles and some very funny stories from the greenfelt jungle. "Some of the best advice you'll ever read on how to win at poker" -- Doyle Brunson. 200 pages, paperback. Originally $19.95, now only $14.95.

**OMAHA HI-LO: Play to Win with the Odds** by Bill Boston. Selecting the right hands to play is the most important decision you'll make in Omaha high-low poker. In this book you'll find the odds for every hand dealt in Omaha high-low—the chances that the hand has of winning the high end of the pot, the low end of it, and how often it is expected to scoop the whole pot. The results are based on 10,000 simulations for each one of the possible 5,211 Omaha high-low hands. Boston has organized the data into an easy-to-use format and added insights learned from years of experience. Learn the 5,211 Omaha high-low hands, the 49 best hands and their odds, the 49 worst hands, trap hands to avoid, and 30 Ace-less hands you can play for profit. A great tool for Omaha players! 156 pages, $19.95.

**OMAHA HI-LO POKER (8 OR BETTER): How to win at the lower limits** by Shane Smith. Since its first printing in 1991, this has become the classic in the field for low-limit players. Readers have lauded the author's clear and concise writing style. Smith shows you how to put players on hands, read the board for high and low, avoid dangerous draws, and use winning betting strategies. Chapters include starting hands, the flop, the turn, the river, and tournament strategy. Illustrated with pictorials of sample hands, an odds chart, and a starting hands chart. Lou Krieger, author of Poker for Dummies, says, Shane Smith's book is terrific! If you're new to Omaha high-low split or if you're a low-limit player who wants to improve your game, you ought to have this book in your poker library. Complex concepts are presented in an easy-to-understand format. It's a gem! 82 pages, spiralbound. $17.95.

**THE WACKY SIDE OF POKER** by Ralph E. Wheeler. Take a walk on the wacky side with 88 humorous poker cartoons! Also includes 220 wise and witty poker quotes. Lighten up from all the heavy reading and preparation of the games wit a quick walk through this fun book. Perfect for holiday gifting. 176 pages filled with wit and wisdom will bring a smile to your face. At less than a ten-spot, you can't go wrong! 176 pages, $9.95.

**Order Toll-Free 1-800-577-WINS or use order form on page 206**

# THE CHAMPIONSHIP SERIES
## POWERFUL BOOKS YOU MUST HAVE

**CHAMPIONSHIP TOURNAMENT POKER** by Tom McEvoy . New Cardoza Edition! Rated by pros as best book on tournaments ever written and enthusiastically endorsed by more than 5 world champions, this is the definitive guide to winning tournaments and a must for every player's library. McEvoy lets you in on the secrets he has used to win millions of dollars in tournaments and the insights he has learned competing against the best players in the world. Packed solid with winning strategies for all 11 games in the World Series of Poker, with extensive discussions of 7-card stud, limit hold'em, pot and no-limit hold'em, Omaha high-low, re-buy, half-half tournaments, satellites, strategies for each stage of tournaments. Tons of essential concepts and specific strategies jam-pack the book. Phil Hellmuth, 1989 WSOP champion says, [this] is the world's most definitive guide to winning poker tournaments. 416 pages, paperback, $29.95.

**CHAMPIONSHIP TABLE (at the World Series of Poker)** by Dana Smith, Ralph Wheeler, and Tom McEvoy. New Cardoza Edition! From 1970 when the champion was presented a silver cup, to the present when the champion was awarded more than $2 million, Championship Table celebrates three decades of poker greats who have competed to win poker's most coveted title. This book gives you the names and photographs of all the players who made the final table, pictures the last hand the champion played against the runner-up, how they played their cards, and how much they won. There is also features fascinating interviews and conversations with the champions and runners-up and interesting highlights from each Series. This is a fascinating and invaluable resource book for WSOP and gaming buffs. In some cases the champion himself wrote "how it happened," as did two-time champion Doyle Brunson when Stu Ungar caught a wheel in 1980 on the turn to deprive "Texas Dolly" of his third title. Includes tons of vintage photographs. 208 pages, paperback, $19.95.

**CHAMPIONSHIP SATELLITE STRATEGY** by Brad Dougherty & Tom McEvoy. In 2002 and 2003 satellite players won their way into the $10,000 WSOP buy-in and emerged as champions, winning more than $2 million each. You can too! You'll learn specific, proven strategies for winning almost any satellite. Learn the 10 ways to win a seat at the WSOP and other big tournaments, how to win limit hold'em and no-limit hold'em satellites, one-table satellites for big tournaments, and online satellites, plus how to play the final table of super satellites. McEvoy and Daugherty sincerely believe that if you practice these strategies, you can win your way into any tournament for a fraction of the buy-in. You'll learn how much to bet, how hard to pressure opponents, how to tell when an opponent is bluffing, how to play deceptively, and how to use your chips as weapons of destruction. Includes a special chapter on no-limit hold'em satellites! 256 pages. illustrated hands, photos, glossary. $24.95.

**CHAMPIONSHIP PRACTICE HANDS** by T. J. Cloutier & Tom McEvoy. Two tournament legends show you how to become a winning tournament player. Get inside their heads as they think they way through the correct strategy at 57 limit and no-limit practice hands. Cloutier & McEvoy show you how to use your skill and intuition to play strategic hands for maximum profit in real tournament scenarios and how 45 key hands were played by champions in turnaround situations at the WSOP. By sharing their analysis on how the winners and losers played key hands, you'll gain tremendous insights into how tournament poker is played at the highest levels. Learn how champions think and how they play major hands in strategic tournament situations, Cloutier and McEvoy believe that you will be able to win your share of the profits in today's tournaments -- and join them at the championship table far sooner than you ever imagined. 288 pages, illustrated with card pictures, $29.95

# THE CHAMPIONSHIP SERIES
## POWERFUL BOOKS YOU MUST HAVE

**CHAMPIONSHIP OMAHA (Omaha High-Low, Pot-limit Omaha, Limit High Omaha)** by T. J. Cloutier & Tom McEvoy. Clearly-written strategies and powerful advice from Cloutier and McEvoy who have won four World Series of Poker titles in Omaha tournaments. Powerful advice shows you how to win at low-limit and high-stakes games, how to play against loose and tight opponents, and the differing strategies for rebuy and freezeout tournaments. Learn the best starting hands, when slowplaying a big hand is dangerous, what danglers are and why winners don't play them, why pot-limit Omaha is the only poker game where you sometimes fold the nuts on the flop and are correct in doing so and overall, how can you win a lot of money at Omaha! 230 pages, photos, illustrations, $39.95.

**CHAMPIONSHIP STUD (Seven-Card Stud, Stud 8/or Better and Razz)** by Dr. Max Stern, Linda Johnson, and Tom McEvoy. The authors, who have earned millions of dollars in major tournaments and cash games, eight World Series of Poker bracelets and hundreds of other titles in competition against the best players in the world show you the winning strategies for medium-limit side games as well as poker tournaments and a general tournament strategy that is applicable to any form of poker. Includes give-and-take conversations between the authors to give you more than one point of view on how to play poker. 200 pages, hand pictorials, photos. $29.95.

**CHAMPIONSHIP HOLD'EM** by T. J. Cloutier & Tom McEvoy. Hard-hitting hold'em the way it's played today in both limit cash games and tournaments. Get killer advice on how to win more money in rammin'-jammin' games, kill-pot, jackpot, shorthanded, and other types of cash games. You'll learn the thinking process before the flop, on the flop, on the turn, and at the river with specific suggestions for what to do when good or bad things happen plus 20 illustrated hands with play-by-play analyses. Specific advice for rocks in tight games, weaklings in loose games, experts in solid games, how hand values change in jackpot games, when you should fold, check, raise, reraise, check-raise, slowplay, bluff, and tournament strategies for small buy-in, big buy-in, rebuy, incremental add-on, satellite and big-field major tournaments. Wow! Easy-to-read and conversational, if you want to become a lifelong winner at limit hold'em, you need this book! 320 Pages, Illustrated, Photos. $39.95

**CHAMPIONSHIP NO-LIMIT & POT LIMIT HOLD'EM** by T. J. Cloutier & Tom McEvoy New Cardoza Edition! The definitive guide to winning at two of the world's most exciting poker games! Written by eight time World Champion players T. J. Cloutier (1998 Player of the Year) and Tom McEvoy (the foremost author on tournament strategy) who have won millions of dollars each playing no-limit and pot-limit hold'em in cash games and major tournaments around the world. You'll get all the answers here - no holds barred - to your most important questions: How do you get inside your opponents' heads and learn how to beat them at their own game? How can you tell how much to bet, raise, and reraise in no-limit hold'em? When can you bluff? How do you set up your opponents in pot-limit hold'em so that you can win a monster pot? What are the best strategies for winning no-limit and pot-limit tournaments, satellites, and supersatellites? You get rock-solid and inspired advice from two of the most recognizable figures in poker — advice that you can bank on. If you want to become a winning player, a champion, you must have this book. 288 pages, paperback, illustrations, photos. $29.95

Order Toll-Free 1-800-577-WINS or use order form on page 206

# POWERFUL POKER SIMULATIONS
## A MUST FOR SERIOUS PLAYERS WITH A COMPUTER!
### IBM compatibles CD ROM Win 95, 98, 2000, NT, ME, XP - Full Color Graphics

**Play interactive poker** against these **incredible** full color poker simulation programs - they're the absolute **best** method to improve game. Computer players act like real players. All games let you set the limits and rake, have fully programmable players, adjustable lineup, stat tracking, and Hand Analyzer for starting hands. Mike Caro, the world's foremost poker theoretician says, "Amazing...A steal for under $500...get it, it's great." Includes free telephone support. **New Feature!** - "Smart advisor" gives expert advice for every play in every game!

**1. TURBO TEXAS HOLD'EM FOR WINDOWS - $89.95** - Choose which players, how many, 2-10, you want to play, create loose/tight game, control check-raising, bluffing, position, sensitivity to pot odds, more! Also, instant replay, pop-up odds, Professional Advisor, keeps track of play statistics. Free bonus: Hold'em Hand Analyzer analyzes all 169 pocket hands in detail, their win rates under any conditions you set. Caro says this "hold'em software is the most powerful ever created." Great product!

**2. TURBO SEVEN-CARD STUD FOR WINDOWS - $89.95** - Create any conditions of play; choose number of players (2-8), bet amounts, fixed or spread limit, bring-in method, tight/loose conditions, position, reaction to board, number of dead cards, stack deck to create special conditions, instant replay. Terrific stat reporting includes analysis of starting cards, 3-D bar charts, graphs. Play interactively, run high speed simulation to test strategies. Hand Analyzer analyzes starting hands in detail. Wow!

**3. TURBO OMAHA HIGH-LOW SPLIT FOR WINDOWS - $89.95** -Specify any playing conditions; betting limits, number of raises, blind structures, button position, aggressiveness/ passiveness of opponents, number of players (2-10), types of hands dealt, blinds, position, board reaction, specify flop, turn, river cards! Choose opponents, use provided point count or create your own. Statistical reporting, instant replay, pop-up odds, high speed simulation to test strategies, amazing Hand Analyzer, much more!

**4. TURBO OMAHA HIGH FOR WINDOWS - $89.95** - Same features as above, but tailored for the Omaha High-only game. Caro says program is "an electrifying research tool...it can clearly be worth thousands of dollars to any serious player. A must for Omaha High players.

**5. TURBO 7 STUD 8 OR BETTER - $89.95** - Brand new with all the features you expect from the Wilson Turbo products: the latest artificial intelligence, instant advice and exact odds, play versus 2-7 opponents, enhanced data charts that can be exported or printed, the ability to fold out of turn and immediately go to the next hand, ability to peek at opponents hand, optional warning mode that warns you if a play disagrees with the advisor, and automatic testing mode that can run up to 50 tests unattended. Challenge tough computer players who vary their styles for a truly great poker game.

### 6. TOURNAMENT TEXAS HOLD'EM - $59.95

Set-up for tournament practice and play, this realistic simulation pits you against celebrity look-alikes. Tons of options let you control tournament size with 10 to 300 entrants, select limits, ante, rake, blind structures, freezeouts, number of rebuys and competition level of opponents - average, tough, or toughest. Pop-up status report shows how you're doing vs. the competition. Save tournaments in progress to play again later. Additional feature allows

# CARDOZA SCHOOL OF BLACKJACK
## - Home Instruction Course - $200 OFF! -

**At last**, after years of secrecy, the **previously unreleased** lesson plans, strategies and playing tactics formerly available only to members of the Cardoza School of Blackjack are now available to the general public - and at substantial savings. **Now**, you can **learn at home,** and at your own convenience. Like the full course given at the school, the home instruction course goes **step-by-ste**p over the winning concepts. We'll take you from layman to **pro**.

**MASTER BLACKJACK** - Learn what it takes to be a **master player**. Be a **power-house**, play with confidence, impunity, and **with the odds** on your side. Learn to be a **big winner** at blackjack.

**MAXIMIZE WINNING SESSIONS** - You'll **learn how** to take a good winning session and make a **blockbuster** out of it, but just as important, you'll learn to cut your losses. Learn exactly when to end a session. We cover everything from the psychological and emotional aspects of play to altered playing conditions (through the **eye of profitability**) to protection of big wins. The advice here could be worth **hundreds (or thousands) of dollars** in one session alone. Take our guidelines seriously.

**ADVANCED STRATEGIES** - You'll learn the latest in advanced winning strategies. Learn about the **ten-factor**, the **Ace-factor**, the effects of rules variations, how to protect against dealer blackjacks, the winning strategies for single and multiple deck games and how each affects you; the **true count**, the multiple deck true count variations, and much, much more. And, of course, you'll receive the full Cardoza Base Count Strategy package.

**$200 OFF - LIMITED OFFER** - The Cardoza School of Blackjack home instruction course, retailed at $295 (or $895 if taken at the school) is available here for just $95.

**DOUBLE BONUS!** - **Rush** your order in **now**, for we're also including, **absolutely free**, the 1,000 and 1,500 word essays, "How to Disguise the Fact that You're an Expert", and "How Not to Get Barred". Among other **inside information** contained here, you'll learn about the psychology of the pit bosses, how they spot counters, how to project a losing image, role playing, and other skills to maximize your profit potential.

To order, send $95 (plus postage and handling) by check or money order to:
    Cardoza Publishing, P.O. Box 1500, Cooper Station, New York, NY 10276

# VIDEOS BY MIKE CARO
## THE MAD GENIUS OF POKER

### CARO'S PRO POKER TELLS

The long-awaited two-video set is a powerful scientific course on how to use your opponents' gestures, words and body language to read their hands and win all their money. These carefully guarded poker secrets, filmed with 63 poker notables, will revolutionize your game. It reveals when opponents are bluffing, when they aren't, and why. Knowing what your opponent's gestures mean, and protecting them from knowing yours, gives you a huge winning edge. An absolute must buy! $59.95.

### CARO'S MAJOR POKER SEMINAR

The legendary "Mad Genius" is at it again, giving poker advice in VHS format. This new tape is based on the inaugural class at Mike Caro University of Poker, Gaming and Life strategy. The material given on this tape is based on many fundamentals introduced in Caro's books, papers, and articles and is prepared in such a way that reinforces concepts old and new. Caro's style is easy-going but intense with key concepts stressed and re-peated. This tape will improve your play. 60 Minutes. $24.95.

### CARO'S POWER POKER SEMINAR

This powerful video shows you how to win big money using the little-known concepts of world champion players. This advice will be worth thousands of dollars to you every year, even more if you're a big money player! After 15 years of refusing to allow his seminars to be filmed, Caro presents entertaining but serious coverage of his long-guarded secrets. Contains the most profitable poker advice ever put on video. 62 Minutes! $39.95.

**Order Toll-Free 1-800-577-WINS or use order form on page 206**

# BOOKS BY MIKE CARO
## THE MAD GENIUS OF POKER

**CARO'S BOOK OF TELLS (THE BODY LANGUAGE OF POKER)** - Finally! Mike Caro's classic book is now revised and back in print! This long-awaited revision by the Mad Genius of Poker takes a detailed look at the art and science of tells, the physical mannerisms which giveaway a player's hand. Featuring photo illustrations of poker players in action along with Caro's explanations about when players are bluffing and when they're not, these powerful eye-opening ideas can give you the decisive edge at the table! This invaluable book should be in every player's library! 352 pages! $24.95.

**CARO'S GUIDE TO DOYLE BRUNSON'S SUPER SYSTEM** - Working with World Champion Doyle Brunson, the legendary Mike Caro has created a fresh look to the "Bible" of all poker books, adding new and personal insights that help you understand the original work. Caro breaks 36 concepts into either "Analysis, Commentary, Concept, Mission, Play-By-Play, Psychology, Statistics, Story, or Strategy. Lots of illustrations and winning concepts give even more value to this great work. 86 pages, 8 1/2 x 11, stapled. $19.95.

**CARO'S FUNDAMENTAL SECRETS OF WINNING POKER** - The world's foremost poker theoretician and strategist presents the essential strategies, concepts, and secret winning plays that comprise the very foundation of winning poker play. Shows how to win more from weak players, equalize stronger players, bluff a bluffer, win big pots, where to sit against weak players, the six factors of strategic table image. Includes selected tips on hold 'em, 7 stud, draw, lowball, tournaments, more. 160 Pages, 5 1/2 x 8 1/2, perfect bound, $12.95.

Call Toll Free (800)577-WINS or Use Coupon Below to Order Books, Videos & Software

## BECOME A BETTER POKER PLAYER!

YES! I want to be a winner! Rush me the following items: (Write in choices below):

| Quantity | Your Book Order | Price | |
|---|---|---|---|
| | | | |
| | | | |
| | | | |
| | | | |
| | | | |
| | | | |
| | Subtotal | | |
| | Postage/Handling: First Item | $5 | 00 |
| | Additional Postage | | |
| | Total Amount Due | | |

**MAKE CHECKS TO:**
**Cardoza Publishing**
P.O. Box 1500
Cooper Station
New York, NY 10276

**CHARGE BY PHONE:**
Toll-Free:     1-800-577-WINS
E-Mail Orders: cardozapub@aol.com

SHIPPING CHARGES: For US orders, include $5.00 postage/handling 1st book ordered; for each additional book, add $1.00. For Canada/Mexico, double above amounts, quadruple (4X) for all other countries. Orders outside U.S., money order payable in U.S. dollars on U.S. bank only.

NAME _____

ADDRESS _____

CITY _____ STATE _____ ZIP _____

**30 day money back guarantee!**

Champ Table

# DOYLE BRUNSON'S SUPER SYSTEM
## A COURSE IN POKER POWER!
### by World Champion Doyle Brunson

**CONSIDERED BY PROS THE BEST POKER BOOK EVER WRITTEN**
This is the **classic** book on every major no-limit game played today and is considered by the pros to be one of the **best books ever written** on poker! **Jam-packed** with **advanced strategies**, theories, tactics and money-making techniques - no serious poker player can afford to be without this **essential** book! Hardbound, and packed with 605 pages of hard-hitting information, this is truly a **must-buy** for aspiring pros. Includes 50 pages of the most precise poker statistics ever published!

**CHAPTERS WRITTEN BY GAME'S SUPERSTARS**
The best theorists and poker players in the world, Dave Sklansky, Mike Caro, Chip Reese, Bobby Baldwin and Doyle Brunson, a book by champions for aspiring pros - cover the **essential** strategies and **advanced play** in their respective specialties. Three world champions and two master theorists and players provide non-nonsense winning advice on making money at the tables.

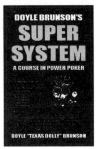

**LEARN WINNING STRATEGIES FOR THE MAJOR POKER GAMES**
The important money games today are covered in depth by these **poker superstars**. You'll learn seven-card stud, draw poker, lowball, seven-card low stud (razz), high-low split (cards speak) and high-low declare; and the most popular game in the country today, hold'em (limit and no-limit). Each game is covered in detail with the **important winning concepts** and strategies clearly explained so that anyone can become a **bigger money** winner.

**SERIOUS POKER PLAYERS MUST HAVE THIS BOOK**
This is **mandatory reading** for aspiring poker pros, players planning to enter tournaments, players ready to play no-limit. Doyle Brunson's Super System is also ideal for average players seeking to move to higher stakes games for bigger wins and more challenges.

To order, send $29.95 by check or money order to Cardoza Publishing